This bite-sized bo
a useful overview
achieve the follo

- Understand
- Identify the __
- Explore ways to be kind to others
- Recognise the value of self-kindness
- Make a positive difference

Kind people are the best
kind of people

Unknown

Being kind

Being kind is an important way of bringing meaning to your own life as well as bringing joy and happiness to the lives of those around you. It is a way that you can spread goodness in the world and make a positive difference.

Kindness is the innate ability we all share as human beings and is defined as the quality of being friendly, generous, and considerate. It is also about being affectionate, gentle, warm, and caring. Being kind allows you to communicate better, be more compassionate, and also to be a positive force in the world.

Kindness can become its
own motive.
We are made kind by
being kind

Eric Hoffer

Benefits of kindness

There are many benefits of kindness and when you are kind to others, you will feel happier. Think about the last time you did something kind for someone else. How did it make you feel?

Kindness, in many ways, is a mindset and a choice and something everyone can engage in. You can ultimately choose the way you want to behave in every given situation.

Here are a few reasons why kindness is so important and some of the key benefits:

Do your little bit of good
where you are; it's those little
bits of good put together that
overwhelm the world

Desmond Tutu

Kindness is contagious

When you see someone do something kind or thoughtful, or you find yourself on the receiving end of kindness, it can inspire you to be kinder to yourself. In this way, kindness spreads from one person to the next, influencing the behaviour of people who perhaps didn't even witness the original act. It is the glue that connects people and it is the key to supporting a healthier, happier and psychologically safer world.

Random acts of kindness can be as small as smiling at a stranger, visiting someone who you know is lonely, or telling someone how much they mean to you. Other ways could be holding a door open or giving up your seat on a busy train. It is these moments that spark a chain reaction of kindness in people around you.

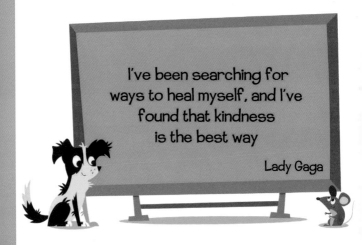

I've been searching for
ways to heal myself, and I've
found that kindness
is the best way

Lady Gaga

Kindness is good for your health

When you are kind, a hormone called oxytocin is released into your body and oxytocin triggers a release of nitric oxide. This chemical then dilutes your blood cells and shrinks inflammation in the cardiovascular system, which in turn reduces blood pressure and the chances of heart disease.

This is just one of the multiple benefits of kindness and, according to the Mental Health Foundation, helping others is actually beneficial for your own mental health and well-being. Being kind can help reduce stress and improve your emotional well-being and physical health.

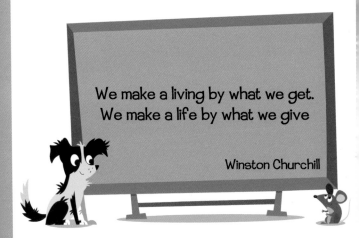

We make a living by what we get.
We make a life by what we give

Winston Churchill

Kindness improves confidence

Kindness can make you feel good about yourself and improve your self-confidence. It can help to increase your sense of self-worth and self-belief, which will have a big impact on your confidence.

Kindness is a positive mental state and it is about giving and being open to others. The act of giving returns a sense of well-being and connection that improves your own emotional state. Being kind is in itself a powerful and consistent reward and self-esteem booster.

Wherever there is a human being, there is an opportunity for kindness

Seneca

Kindness combats loneliness

One of the kindest things we can do for another human being is to help them feel less alone. To be truly happy, humans need intimate bonds and to be able to confide in each other and feel supported.

One small act of kindness can make a huge impact on someone else's life. When people feel lost and alone, kind actions help restore faith and in turn can bring hope to entire communities. This could start with a smile or a caring conversation.

A story about kindness

One day a man was sitting by a river, watching a scorpion floundering around in the water. He decided to save it by stretching out his finger, but the scorpion stung him. The man still tried to help the scorpion out of the water, but the scorpion stung him again.

A passer-by saw what he was doing and asked him why he was trying to save the scorpion when it kept stinging him. The man simply replied: "It is the nature of the scorpion to sting. It is my nature to love. Why should I give up my nature to love just because it is the nature of the scorpion to sting?"

Love anyway

The message here is to not give up your loving nature and kind heart even if other people around may hurt you. It is inevitable that people will do that, sometimes with intention and other times without even being aware of it through carelessness or insensitivity. When people are not very nice it is often because they are unhappy.

A loving and compassionate heart is a far more constructive way to deal with something or someone than to feel bitter and resentful. Being loving and focusing on kindness will bring you far more peace and happiness. It may even rub off!

Kindness is a language
which the deaf can hear
and the blind can see

Mark Twain

How to
be kind

To be kind to others you must
first be kind to yourself

Unknown

Be kind to yourself

Self-care and self-compassion are so important when it comes to being healthy, happy and resilient. Investing in your personal well-being is kindness in itself because when you feel better about yourself you will set a positive example, which will positively influence others to be kind to themselves too.

It is also important not to judge yourself harshly for not being perfect or making mistakes and letting your inner critic make you feel bad. Holding yourself to impossibly high standards or comparing yourself to unrealistic role models in the pursuit of perfectionism is not helpful. You are a unique person and you were not born to be perfect anyway, you were born to be real. So be your own best friend and be kind to yourself.

We are what we repeatedly do.
Excellence, then, is not an act,
but a habit

Aristotle

Make kindness a habit

You are essentially what you repeatedly do and in many ways kindness is a habit and is one that everyone can cultivate. A great way to build the habit is to focus on kindness every day for a month. Set out to do kind things for yourself and for others. Then set aside time at the end of each day to reflect and write down some of the things that you have done.

At the end of this directed focus, you will start to become more aware of profound changes in your life. You will feel better about yourself as a person in the knowledge that you are making a positive difference.

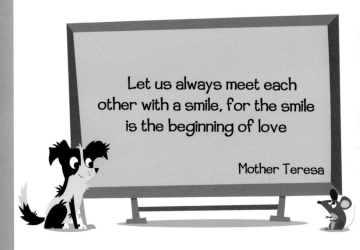

Let us always meet each
other with a smile, for the smile
is the beginning of love

Mother Teresa

Be friendly

Most kind people have a tendency to be genuinely friendly. This doesn't mean that you have to be the most outgoing person in the room, it is more about making an effort to get to know people and to make them feel as if you care.

For example, if there is someone in an environment that is new to them, explaining how things work or inviting them to a social event may help them. Even just smiling and making small talk with people can go a long way in making you friendlier. Positive human connection is so important and can have such a profound impact.

Gift people your time

Time is a very precious commodity and giving people your time is a valuable gift. Being truly present and listening to someone, by avoiding all distractions and giving a person the time of day, is one of the greatest acts of kindness. Take the time to truly absorb yourself in what the other person is saying, before responding and demonstrate to the person that you appreciate their unique situation.

Being a good listener doesn't mean being a great problem solver. Sometimes, the best thing you can do is just be there. There are times when we all appreciate a good listening to!

Be compassionate

Sometimes, people may not be very nice to you and it could well upset you. It is always worth reminding yourself that often this is born out of unhappiness, insecurity, loneliness, stress or fatigue. Extending the hand of human kindness in these situations can be challenging, although this is the time when people need your kindness the most.

It can be easy to lose sight of that when you are embroiled in your own problems or if you are upset with them. Before you react in a way that might have a negative impact on the other person, stop and ask yourself – is this the kindest response? Then make a choice to respond with compassion.

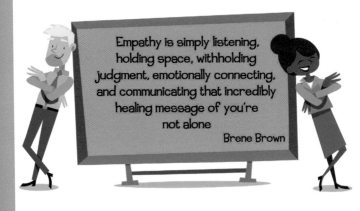

Empathy is simply listening, holding space, withholding judgment, emotionally connecting, and communicating that incredibly healing message of you're not alone

Brene Brown

Empathise

Empathy and understanding are part of an emotional process that builds connection between people. It is about 'reading' another person's inner state and interpreting it in a way that will help the other person to feel supported and it also has the added benefit of developing mutual trust.

To truly empathise and understand another individual is an intuitive act where you need to give complete attention to the other person's experience and push your own issues aside. By helping someone feel secure enough to open up and share their experience will help them to establish perspective. This, in turn, is a kind way of helping people to feel better and happier.

Gossip is the Devil's radio

George Harrison

Avoid gossip

Social media can be a playground for toxic behaviour and a place where gossip-mongering is rife. Even just reading some of the cruel and unnecessarily hurtful comments about other people fuels the bandwagon and can contaminate your own thinking.

Being critical, judgmental and gossiping about other people is not about kindness. You will feel much happier when you actively seek out the good in people and practise tolerance and empathy. If you haven't got something positive, helpful or constructive to say about someone else it is better to say nothing.

Be optimistic

Be optimistic and seek out the good in others and in the world around you. This will also help you to be resilient and deal with adversity and life's inevitable setbacks. Optimism is the bedrock of kindness and will continuously restore your faith in humanity.

Cultivating an optimistic outlook and a positive mindset will ensure that acts of kindness are delivered with genuine joy rather than with reluctance or out of a sense of duty.

Be grateful

Cultivating an attitude of gratitude is a fundamental part of being kind. It is so important not to take anything for granted and thank people and let them know how much you appreciate them.

Kind people are easily able to express gratitude and make a habit of being more grateful. If you are more observant of all the kind things other people do for you, then you will be more ready to do kind things for others. Being aware of how good the kindness of others makes you feel will fuel your desire to be kinder.

We do not inherit the Earth
from our ancestors.

We borrow it from our children

Indian proverb

Be kind to the planet

Climate change is impacting our planet and raising awareness of how much waste you can potentially create and how much damage that wreaks is a good place to start to counteract it. If every individual and every business made an effort to reduce their impact on the environment then together a real difference can be made. The changes that you make don't have to be huge either and there are so many simple things that you can do at home or in the workplace that will help to save the planet.

Making a conscious habit of eliminating one-use plastic, saving water, turning off lights or thinking twice before you drive your car instead of cycling or walking can make such an important impact. All of these actions will positively contribute towards reducing factors such as carbon emissions and greenhouse gases, as well as saving you money. You will also be rich in the knowledge that you are an eco warrior rather than an eco wrecker!

What this world needs is
a new kind of army-
the army of the kind

Cleveland Amory

Join the kindness revolution

In a world that can sometimes be cruel and unkind, it is time to start a revolution ... A kindness revolution!

Wherever possible (and it is always possible), be kind. Every day of your life there will be ways you can practise kindness. So go out there and discover what they are. Life is a precious gift and every living human being has the opportunity to make a positive difference.

Building a culture of kindness

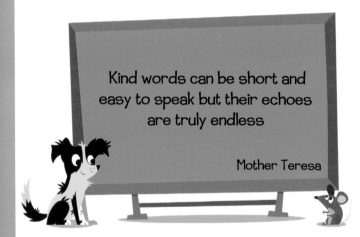

Kind words can be short and easy to speak but their echoes are truly endless

Mother Teresa

Ways to be kind

There are so many ways that you can demonstrate kindness and here are a few small things that you can do that can make someone else's day, including your own!

- Say hello and smile at a passer-by
- Make someone laugh
- Pick up litter as you walk
- Buy an unexpected gift for someone
- Let someone in a queue go before you
- Volunteer for charity
- Organise a fundraising event
- Give blood
- Listen to someone else's concerns
- Choose your words kindly

Ways to be kind

- Give someone a hug
- Deliver some positive feedback
- Tell someone how much they mean to you
- Send someone a card
- Pass on a book you've enjoyed
- Declutter and donate to charity
- Forgive someone who has hurt you
- Visit someone who is lonely
- Tidy up after yourself
- Hold a door open for someone
- Help someone who is lost
- Offer to babysit a child or a pet
- Give yourself a hug

Three things
in human life are important:
the first is to be kind;
the second is to be kind;
and the third is to be kind

Henry James

Explore more kindness

The following websites have been a very useful resource for researching and compiling this bite-sized book. There are some wonderful initiatives going on in the world and there is a wealth of information to explore.

- www.actionforhappiness.org
- www.thegreatkindnesschallenge.com
- www.kindspring.org
- www.thriveglobal.com
- www.randomactsofkindness.org
- www.greatergood.berkeley.edu
- www.charterforcompassion.org
- www.spreadkindness.org
- www.theworldkindnessmovement.org

Miami

- A  in the text denotes a highly recommended sight
- A complete A–Z of practical information starts on p.105
- Extensive mapping on cover flaps and throughout text

Berlitz Publishing Company, Inc.

Princeton   Mexico City   Dublin   Eschborn   Singapore

Text: Elizabeth Brown
Photography: Aram Gesar; Jacques Bétant
Cover photo: ©1998 David Friske
Layout: Media Content Marketing, Inc.
Cartography: ⊕ Falk-Verlag, Munich

We are particularly grateful to Jay Clarke and the staff of the
Greater Miami Convention & Visitors Bureau for their help in
the preparation of this book.

Although the publisher tries to insure the accuracy of all the
information in this book, changes are inevitable and errors may
result. The publisher cannot be responsible for any resulting loss,
inconvenience, or injury. If you find an error in this guide, please
let the editors know by writing to Berlitz Publishing Company,
400 Alexander Park, Princeton, NJ 08540-6306.

ISBN 2-8315-6975-3

Revised 1998 – Second Printing June 1999

Printed in Italy
029/906 RP

CONTENTS

MIAMI

THE CITY AND
ITS PEOPLE

Miami's geographical and cultural position brings a unique flavour to the great American tradition of cosmopolitan life. The largest city of Florida, it has become in many ways the northernmost city of Latin America.

Tallahassee runs Florida's state government and bureaucracy, but there's no doubt in anybody's mind that Greater Miami is the state's major centre for commerce, culture, and sheer urban bounce. Up in the gleaming glass-and-steel skyscrapers of the banking and business districts, the city provides a vital link in financial relations between North and South America. Down in the streets, Miami offers delicatessens and supper clubs reminiscent of New York and New Jersey, strong Cuban coffee and cigars, and the exotic beat of Caribbean music.

This is the place where the sun spends the winter, a subtropical haven that never sees the snow. Even in January, the coolest month here, thermometers average around 23°C (74° F), while the trade winds temper the summer highs. With a good hat and the right lotions, you can enjoy this town all year round.

The city stands at the mouth of the Miami River on the shore of Biscayne Bay. Greater Miami's metropolitan area comprises 26 municipalities, which sprawl between the Everglades swamps and the Atlantic Ocean. Almost half the metropolitan region's population of more than 2 million are of Latin-American or Caribbean origin.

For visitors, the city is most famous for the bright and breezy hotels of its resort area, South Beach, connected to the mainland by causeways. But massive construction, at a cost of billions of dollars, has given a dramatic new look to the downtown district, attracting business people and shoppers as well as visitors taking time away from the beaches. Sleek office towers line Flagler Street, Biscayne Boulevard, and Brickell Avenue, the Wall Street of the South. More than 200 million dollars were spent on the First Union Financial Center alone, the tallest structure south of New York and east of Houston. With completion of the Bayside leisure complex and the ultra-modern "peoplemover" (elevated train) system, renaissance in Miami beyond South Beach is becoming a reality.

Yet a mere hundred years ago all was wilderness here. A handful of settlers traded with the Indians at the mouth of the Miami River, named by the Tequesta tribe to mean "Big Water." The pioneers lived in part by "wrecking," salvaging the cargoes of ships that ran aground. They also farmed vegetables and citrus fruit for sale in northern markets. Sailing boats from Key West called every fortnight, bringing news of the outside world.

To this frontier outpost came a widow from Ohio named Julia Tuttle. Convinced of South Florida's potential for development, she urged railway magnate Henry Flagler to expand his Florida East Coast line south to Miami. At first the tycoon refused, but Mrs. Tuttle persisted. Finally, in 1896, the railway reached Miami, Flagler built a luxury hotel on Biscayne Bay, and Miami's course was set.

The resilient city has weathered killer hurricanes and financial collapse, the panic of the 1962 missile crisis, and the big-city woes of riots and drug traffic. The Miami authorities seem now to have their problems well under control.

Things are looking up for Miami Beach, too. Hugely popular in the 1920s and 1930s, and again in the 1950s and 1960s, the resort is bounding back in favour as a new generation of holidaymakers discovers the pleasures of the "Florida Riviera," with its silver sands and swaying palms.

Fun-loving Miamians bring simple recreations, such as skating, to a higher level.

Certain parts remain a largely Jewish enclave and a retirement haven from the chills of the north. Preservationists are restoring the Jazz Age hotels that line Ocean Drive in the Art Deco District, a national historic area and the heart of a youthful area with a large gay population, known as South Beach (or SoBe to those in the know). The famous resort palaces along Collins Avenue are also undergoing extensive remodelling.

The beach itself is bigger and better than before. The tide was lapping at the gateposts of the oceanfront hotels when the United States Army Corps of Engineers created a new strand stretching 100 metres (300 feet) to the high-water line. Now, as in the 1920s, there's a boardwalk by the sea.

Little Havana, south of downtown, provides a focus for Miami's thriving Hispanic community. The Spanish language dominates Calle Ocho, otherwise known to the map-makers as Southwest 8th Street. Cuban grocers display husked coconuts, bundles of sugar cane, piles of avocados, limes, and plantains, mostly Dade County grown. There you can buy Brazilian leather goods, Caribbean herbal cures, and fat "Havana" cigars, hand-rolled in local factories. People from all over the city come to dine on shellfish and *lechón* (roast pork) in Calle Ocho's famous restaurants.

Some 40,000 Haitian refugees have transformed the area around 57th Street and N.E. 2nd Avenue into a Little Haiti. Restaurants and nightclubs with a Creole flavour and a French dialect are opening and reaching out to a larger public.

Coconut Grove is Miami's oldest settlement, pioneered by a resolute band of New England intellectuals before the turn of the century. Yankee individuality has characterized the Grove ever since. Houses turn inward here, buried in lush vegetation, and huge, overarching trees shade bikeways and byways winding down to the bay. Sailing boats crowd the marina, and there are people everywhere, strolling around Florida's prettiest urban village, filling scores of open-air street-side restaurants.

East across the bay is the "Island Paradise" of Key

A monument to Miami's strong connection with Cuba, in Little Havana.

Biscayne, home to one of Miami's best-known tourist attractions, the Seaquarium, and to the popular beaches of Crandon Park and Cape Florida. The University of Miami has its campus in the leafy glades of the city of Coral Gables, while Hialeah lays claim to its namesake, the most beautiful racecourse in the world.

Gambling at the horse and dog races, and at jai-alai games attracts a lot of people to Miami. Speedboat races, regattas, and golf, and tennis tournaments bring many more. But the greatest lure is the great outdoors, the myriad sporting opportunities that Greater Miami offers every month of the year: deep-sea fishing in the Gulf Stream, just offshore; snorkelling, sailing, and windsurfing in the shallow waters of Biscayne Bay; and superb swimming and waterskiing in the warm South Atlantic. Miami's flat terrain is also ideal for jogging, hiking, and cycling.

Shoppers find Miami to be the marketplace for Latin America. The Fashion District is the place to buy locally manufactured resort clothing and swimwear, while Design District shops stock the best in home furnishings from around the world. In recent years, most of the national department-store chains have expanded their operations to Greater Miami. Bloomingdale's, Saks, and Neiman Marcus are here.

Top attractions on the tourist circuit include the aforementioned Seaquarium, and Miccosukee Indian Village. Miami's most stately home, Vizcaya, is a must on any itinerary, as are the excellent shows at the Miami Art Museum. Among the many opportunities for day trips, an excursion to the Everglades is the one definitely not to be missed.

By way of an evening's entertainment, there's the glamour of a Latin supper club, or the glitter of a South Beach nightspot. An international roster of jazz, pop, and rock

Miami's beaches offer crowds, warm water, fine sand, and plenty of sunshine.

artists appears at the Gusman Cultural Center, the Knight Center, Dade County Auditorium, and other venues all over town. Avant-garde music and dance, opera, theatre, and musicals—all get an airing in Greater Miami.

Eating out means eating ethnic fare, sampling the best of a dozen different cuisines, from Cuban to Creole, or enjoying an ever expanding universe of chic restaurants serving everything from French cuisine to those specialities of Greater Miami, sweet Florida stone crabs and creamy Key lime pie.

Perhaps the biggest event of the Miami year is the King Orange Festival and its climax on New Year's Eve, the King Orange Jamboree Parade, largest nighttime march in the world. On or near January 6, Little Havana stages its own annual

Three King's Parade, complete with floats and marching bands. The Grand Prix motor race draws throngs of people to Biscayne Boulevard in late February and early March, and Carnaval Miami ushers in the Lenten season in exuberant Latin style. A series of festivals highlights Miami's exciting cultural diversity—the Italian Renaissance Festival at Vizcaya, the Bahamas Goombay Festival in Coconut Grove, and the Miccosukee Indian Annual Arts Festival.

Every year, Greater Miami is a magnet for nearly 10 million visitors. And the number is rising, as people from all over find fresh stimulation under the southern sun.

Greater Miami at a Glance

Geography: Area 5,462 sq km (2,109 square miles), including 139 sq km (54 square miles) of water, extensive farmland, and Everglades swampland. The greater metropolis incorporates Miami and Miami Beach and 24 other municipalities.

Population: More than 2 million (Anglo 40%, Hispanic 45%, Black 15%).

Climate: Winters are warm and sunny, summers hot and humid. Showers can occur late in the afternoon in summer.

Government: Each city has its own local government, which cooperates with the central metropolitan authority (Metro). The city of Miami is the seat of Dade County.

Industries: International banking and trade, tourism, agriculture.

A BRIEF HISTORY

About 4,000 years ago, Indians of Asian origin settled at the mouth of the Miami River. They had come to the end of a journey that brought them from Siberia to Alaska and on across the American continent. Wandering ever southwards, they arrived at last in a land of verdant forests and sunshine, rich in fish and game. And here they lived in splendid isolation until the white man came.

The Spanish explorer Juan Ponce de León discovered Florida in the spring of 1513. He called the peninsula *Pascua florida* after the feast of the flowers during the Easter season. Three months later, Ponce de León sailed down the coast to "Chequescha," the Indian settlement on the Miami River. No one knows for sure whether he stepped ashore, but from that time onwards the Spaniards referred to the Indians residing here as Tequestas.

This primitive yet resourceful people lived in platform houses built of cypress logs and palmetto thatch. They fashioned tools of conch shell and used fish oil to repel insects. The Tequestas were hostile to the white man but less warlike than their neighbours, the Calusas, who attacked and mortally wounded Ponce de León on his return to Florida in 1521.

Territory of Spain

Subsequent attempts at exploration and colonisation failed, and Spain lost interest in Florida with the discovery of gold and silver in Mexico and Peru. In time, other European powers began to compete for territory in the New World. The French established an outpost in north Florida in 1562, but the Spanish soon ousted their rival. King Philip II appointed Pedro Menéndez de Avilés governor and charged him with extending Spanish influence throughout the peninsula.

As luck would have it, Menéndez met up with a fellow countryman on his arrival in Florida. Hernando d'Escalante Fontaneda had survived shipwreck to live with the Indians for 17 years. Versed in their language and familiar with their ways, he served as the governor's interpreter and guide. No sooner did Menéndez pay homage to the chief of the Calusa tribe than the Indian offered his sister to the Spaniard in marriage. "Doña Antonia" thus became Florida's first convert to Christianity— and Menéndez de Avilés the first bigamist. The adventurer was married already to a noblewoman in Spain.

Having won the confidence of the Indians, Menéndez founded the city of St. Augustine in 1565. That same year he established a mission at Tequesta under the auspices of a Jesuit lay worker named Brother Francisco Villareal. Some Spanish mutineers were already in residence when the Jesuit took up his post. Menéndez agreed to pardon them.

All went well for a while. Brother Villareal made a few converts, and the former mutineers constructed a simple fort. Menéndez himself turned up on a tour of inspection. After four days at Fort Tequesta, the governor left for Spain taking several Indians with him. It caused quite a sensation when he had the "noble savages" baptised in the cathedral of Seville.

Back on the Miami River, the Spanish colonists clashed with the Tequestas. There were deaths on both sides before the Europeans made their escape. When the Indian entourage returned from Spain several months later, the mission was reopened, only to be abandoned again in 1570.

The British Take Over

In the long run, contact with the white man was the Tequestas' undoing. European diseases decimated the tribe, and those who survived fell prey to rum or to marauding Creek Indians, who had been pushed down into Florida by British colonial expansion. In 1743, alarmed by Creek incursions and English raids, the Spanish reactivated the fort and mission in south Florida—but not for long, as the Tequestas drove them out. The remaining members of the tribe fled Florida for Cuba when Spain finally ceded the territory to England under the terms of the Treaty of Paris (1763). Creeks called Seminoles, or "wild ones," took possession of the land.

The British tried in vain to attract their countrymen to Florida. A few intrepid settlers arrived by boat from the Bahamas. Known as "Conchs," they lived near the sea, which supplied their larder. Others, known as "Crackers," travelled overland through Georgia to occupy the interior, where they grew collard and mustard greens, their staple diet. Both "Conchs" and "Crackers" stayed on when the territory reverted to Spain in 1783.

A Miccosukee weaver exhibits the products of her craft in Everglade Park.

Under Old Glory

Shortly after the United States annexed Florida in 1821, the population in what is now the state of Florida stood at 317. Agriculture and the wrecking trade developed as settlements took shape at Key West, Indian Key, and Cape Florida on Key Biscayne. To protect shipping, the U.S. government built a lighthouse at Cape Florida in 1826. About the same time, a Carolina planter named Richard Fitzpatrick imported slaves to work a tract of land on the Miami River.

Sparsely settled though South Florida was, virgin land in the East was at a premium as the new United States extended its boundaries outwards across the continent. Congress therefore decreed that Indians remaining on the seaboard be transferred to reservations in the West. The Removal Act of 1830 had serious repercussions in Florida, sparking the long and bitter Second and Third Seminole Wars.

The Indians had already skirmished with American frontiersmen before Spain relinquished control of Florida. General Andrew Jackson himself rode victorious into the fray, dislodging Seminoles from the north to the centre of the peninsula, opening new territory to development. In December 1835, Indians massacred an army unit on manoeuvres between Tampa and Ocala. Seminoles in Miami took up arms a month later, murdering a family in residence on the Fitzpatrick plantation. They went on to burn the lighthouse at Cape Florida the following July. The United States army sent troops to Miami in 1839, as Seminole raids continued. The soldiers were billeted at Fort Dallas on the Miami River, in barracks established by the Navy a few years before. Chekika, chief of the tribe, personally led an attack on Indian Key which left seven dead. The soldiers at Fort Dallas vowed revenge. Dressed like Indians, they surprised Chekika in his Everglades hideaway, killing the chief and a number of his men.

But it was impossible to flush the Seminoles out of the swamp. Bloodhounds were brought over from Cuba to stalk the Indians—a scheme that raised a cry of protest from people throughout the United States—but the dogs kept losing their way in the watery wilderness. The government finally gave up the fight in 1842, bringing the Second Seminole War to an inconclusive end.

That year Richard Fitzpatrick transferred his extensive Miami holdings to his nephew, William English. Filled with enthusiasm for the place, English mapped out a village he called Miami on the south bank of the river, advertising lots for sale for $1 each. The government offered free land to anyone who would hold it by force of arms for five years, and some stout souls carved out homesteads.

When Florida joined the Union in 1845, people predicted a brilliant future for Miami—until the Indians went to war again in 1855. A contingent of soldiers arrived to root out the recalcitrant Seminoles, and Fort Dallas was expanded. Between missions, the men built roads and bridges in the wilderness around Miami. After two years of fighting, all but a few hundred Indians had been subdued. That small band withdrew deep into the Everglades as the third and final Seminole War drew to a close.

Frontier Town

Deserters, spies, and blockade runners frequented the Miami area during the Civil War (1861–1865). Although Florida seceded from the Union, the state saw little bloodshed, and that little was confined to the north. New settlers arrived on the scene when peace returned, boosting the Dade County population to a grand total of 85 by 1870. One of them was William Brickell, who set up a trading post at the mouth of the Miami River. A new era opened as Indians returned to the

Miami settlement to swap alligator skins, egret feathers, and venison for beads, cloth, watches, spirits, and the occasional treadle sewing machine. Meanwhile, thriving agricultural communities grew up at Lemon City, Coconut Grove, Buena Vista, and Little River. These hamlets would one day would be incorporated into the vast metropolis of Greater Miami.

In 1891 a wealthy widow named Julia Tuttle moved to town, setting up home in the rock house that William English had built. She became the biggest landowner in Miami, and over

The swamplands of Florida's Everglades — site of the Second Seminole War.

the next five years was instrumental in getting railway magnate Henry Flagler to build a rail link to the town. On July 28, 1896, with a population of 343, the city was incorporated, taking "Miami" as its name. Streets were laid out, shops and hotels went up, and the Bank of Bay Biscay opened for business.

Resort City

No sooner had Miami taken shape than fire burned it to the ground. The blaze broke out early on Christmas morning, consuming 28 buildings. Luckily, Flagler's sumptuous Royal Palm Hotel escaped destruction. The five-storey, 350-room establishment opened on schedule in January, 1897, a portent of things to come.

Celebrities and notables such as the politician Mark Hanna and meat-packing millionaire Philip Armour found the amenities to their liking, particularly the private yacht dock and swimming pool filled with crystal-clear bay water. Significantly, the hotel hosted its first convention that inaugural season, a gathering of the American Tobacco Growers. By the time the Royal Palm closed for the summer in 1897, Miami was in the tourist business to stay.

On February 7 the following year, just as holidaymakers were returning to town for the winter, the *U.S.S. Maine* was sunk in Havana harbour, precipitating the Spanish-American War. More than 7,000 troops were sent to Miami, as panic seized the city. In August, the conflict ended, as swiftly as it had begun, with the defeat of Spain. The incident brought Miami a lot of good publicity, focusing national attention on the locality as well as introducing some 7,000 potential visitors to the joys of life in the bayfront resort.

Things were barely back to normal when the sudden death of Julia Tuttle stunned the populace on September 14. She was 48. Everyone mourned the "Mother of Miami," whose persistence and perspicacity had brought their community into being. Mrs. Tuttle's son sold the family residence to an entrepreneur who turned it into a gambling casino, though the games of chance were for tourists only.

By 1910, Miami's population topped 5,000. The city had expanded south of the river along bayfront Brickell Avenue, known as "Millionaire's Row" because of its imposing houses. Miami boasted telephones and cars, a fire station, hospital, cinemas, and schools. The city had become a seaport, linked to the Atlantic by Government Cut, a channel dredged to a depth of 6 metres (18 feet).

The continuation of Flagler's Florida East Coast Railway to Homestead and Florida City opened the South Dade pinelands to agriculture. Construction of the final stretch, to Key West, was Flagler's final achievement; a year after the

Julia Tuttle's Dream

Julia Tuttle was no ordinary pioneer, but a visionary of the first order. She pronounced it "the dream of my life to see this wilderness turned into a prosperous country." Mrs. Tuttle confided her dream to railway tycoon Henry Flagler in 1892, entreating him to build his Florida East Coast line south to Miami. She even promised him the title to half her property. But Flagler was involved in the citrus industry in central Florida and in the development of hotels at St. Augustine and Palm Beach. He had no time for new projects.

Two years later, chance played into Mrs. Tuttle's hands. Severe cold weather in the winter of 1894–95 destroyed the citrus crop in central Florida, while subtropical Miami remained free of frost. Mrs. Tuttle sent Flagler a bouquet of orange blossoms to prove the point, renewing her offer of land. Flagler accepted, and in April, 1896, the first train pulled into town.

A bayfront landmark since 1916, palatial Vizcaya brings European flair to the Florida Riviera.

track was completed in 1912, the "Father of Miami" died at the age of 82.

On the Oceanfront

Miami Beach was the haunt of crocodiles when John Collins established an avocado farm beside the sea. As a sideline, the 70-year-old horticulturist founded the Miami Beach Improvement Company. He initiated land sales and began construction of a bridge to the mainland (1912). Work advanced rapidly until Collins ran out of cash. People called the bridge "Collins's Folly." They thought the man had gone mad. At the crucial moment, an entrepreneur from Indiana named Carl Fisher put up all the capital needed in exchange for a wide swath of oceanfront land.

Fisher had plans of his own for Miami Beach. He cleared away the palmettos and mangroves and went on to create new acreage by dredging the shallow bay. While war raged in Europe, "America's Winter Playground" took shape, complete with golf courses, tennis courts and polo fields. The U.S. declaration of hostilities halted construction for a while, but business activity picked up quickly once the armistice was signed on 11 November 1918.

Boom and Bust

In an era of easy money and changing moral values, people flooded into Miami and land sales boomed. Developer George Merrick sold the first lot in his "Master Suburb" of Coral Gables in 1921. At first it seemed an unlikely venture, since the site was so far from town, but within a year Coral Gables property transactions totalled as much as $1,400,000.

As demand for land increased, plots as far as 13 km (eight miles) beyond the Miami city limits fetched prices of $20,000 an acre and more. Bay sites slated for reclamation were sold "by the gallon." Some salesmen didn't bother with land at all; speculating on spiralling prices, they traded in "binders"—five or ten per cent deposits paid in advance of final sale.

Some unscrupulous estate agents gave the area a bad name, further blackened by the rising incidence of crime, some of it prohibition-related. The situation got so far out of hand by 1925 that the Ku Klux Klan offered to step in and keep the peace. City officials politely declined.

The boom was already losing momentum when a devastating hurricane hit Miami in September 1926. Not a building escaped unscathed, with damage running to millions of dollars. Townspeople were still picking up the pieces when the stock market crash of 1929 triggered the Great Depression. Scores of local businesses went bankrupt and every Miami bank but one defaulted.

Boom Again

Recovery came earlier to Miami than to most American cities. Pan American Airways and Eastern Airlines had both begun to operate out of Miami, and during the 1937–1938 season around 800,000 visitors vacationed here. As a result of the boom, hundreds of new hotels in streamlined style went up on the south shore of Miami Beach, in the area preserved today as the Art Deco District, in the heart of the booming neighborhood of South Beach.

War and its Aftermath

World War II brought big changes to Miami. The Air Force and Navy opened military training camps in Miami and Miami Beach; golf courses and beaches were turned into drill grounds, and hotels were commandeered as barracks.

Blue waters and white skyscrapers—a line of sand separates the two along Miami Beach.

24

WHERE TO GO

Greater Miami combines the pleasures of resort life with all the urban excitement a tourist could wish for. From a base by the seaside—be it Key Biscayne, Miami Beach, Surfside, Bal Harbour, or Sunny Isles—it's easy to make forays across the bay into the greater metropolis.

There's no better introduction to Miami than a ride on the Metrorail, the elevated public-transport system. The line crosses every ethnic and economic boundary in the city as it travels from suburban South Dade to the centre and on through Miami's northern neighbourhoods.

Come sail away—sailboats cluster around the marina at Coconut Grove.

We begin our tour of Greater Miami "downtown," in the city of Miami, the expanding business and cultural hub of the metropolitan area. After a look at the bayfront, port, and Brickell Avenue financial district, we enter the Cuban enclave of Little Havana. Then it's on to the "City Beautiful" of Coral

Getting Around

At first glance Miami seems a confusing urban sprawl, crossed by a bewildering profusion of expressways. On closer acquaintance, the logic of the town plan becomes clear. Laid out on a grid, Miami divides into four sections: northeast, northwest, southeast, southwest. Flagler Street in the city of Miami serves as the boundary between north and south' Miami Avenue between east and west. The eastern quadrants of town cover a relatively small area, while the western sections have expanded out towards the Everglades—far beyond the limits foreseen by Miami's pioneers. Addresses will be easier to find if you remember that an avenue, road, place, or court runs north–south, and that a street, terrace, or alley has an east–west orientation.

Outside rush hours (7:00 to 9:00 a.m. and 4:00 to 6:00 p.m.), the expressway system speeds cross-town journeys. The main north–south arteries include the North–South Expressway (also known as Interstate-95, or I-95), which travels from the southwest section right through the city and on up the state. The Palmetto Expressway, sometimes referred to as State Road (SR) 826, goes from South Dade to North Miami. The Florida Turnpike Extension (SR 821) links Homestead and Florida City to northern Dade County. For through journeys, it's best to avoid the congested national north–south highway, US 1, known locally as the Dixie Highway.

For east–west trips, take the Dolphin Expressway (SR 836)—which runs just south of the airport to the North–South Expressway—or the Airport Expressway (SR 112), which connects the terminal to Miami Beach via the Julia Tuttle Causeway.

Gables and trendy Coconut Grove, a Floridian Greenwich Village. There's just time for a taste of bohemia before we cross over to the Beaches: the lush isle of Key Biscayne; glamorous, garish Miami Beach and its newest, trendiest enclave, South Beach; friendly Surfside; exclusive Bal Harbour; and popular Sunny Isles.

The scene changes abruptly as we head out through the southern suburbs to the pineland and hammocks of Everglades National Park, where signposted footpaths penetrate deep into the tropical wilderness. To reach the northern sector of the park, we return to town and follow Tamiami Trail west past the hamlet of Coopertown to Shark Valley in the open glades, scene of biking, hiking, and tram expeditions, water levels permitting. Last stop on our Everglades itinerary is farther down the Trail: the reservation of the Miccosukee Indians.

Among other sightseeing possibilities we propose are tourist attractions such as the Seaquarium and Parrot Jungle, historical sights that include The Barnacle and Coral Gables House, and museums such as Vizcaya and the Historical Museum of South Florida. Choose from our selection according to your interests, referring to the map on pages 30 and 31.

GREATER MIAMI

There's a lot of territory to cover on the mainland of Miami, beginning with the reviving city centre.

Downtown

A generation ago, residents abandoned Miami proper for suburbia, and the city fell into decline. Now the focus is shifting back to the centre. If you think of downtown as an area to avoid, you're decidedly out of date, though it's still an area best visited during weekdays, when its banks and other businesses provide a lively urban pace that is decidedly

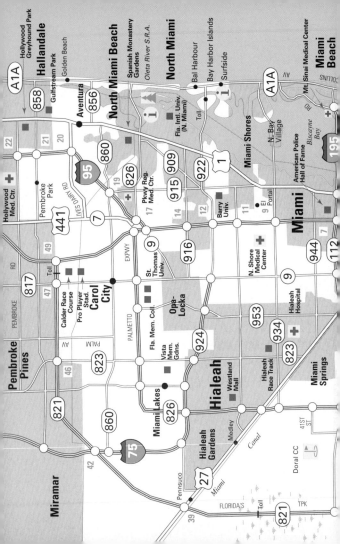

MIAMI AND MIAMI BEACH

Fisher Island

Virginia Key

Miami Marine Stadium

Miami Seaquarium

Crandon Golf at
Key Biscayne

Crandon Park

Key Biscayne

Key Biscayne

Bill Baggs
Cape Florida
State Rec. Area

N

Mus. of Science

Vizcaya Mus.

Mercy Hospital

Coconut Grove
Playhouse

Barnacle
S.H.S.

Intracoastal Waterway

Biscayne Bay

**Coral
Gables**

Healthsouth Larkin Hospital

Fairchild
Tropical
Garden

Chicken Key

Pan Am Hosp.

Youth
Mus.

**West
Miami**

Venetian
Pool

Lowe
Art Mus.

Univ. of
Miami

South Miami

Dadeland
Mall

Parrot Jungle

Kendall

972

976

826

DR

HOWARD

1

Rockdale

CUTLER RD

Miami Intl. Expo Ctr.

Florida
Intl. Univ.
(Univ. Park)

Art Museum
at FIU

**Westwood
Lake**

973

985

986

94

KENDA

DR

Baptist Hosp.
of Miami

**Richmond
Hts.**

Gold Coast
Railroad Mus.

Thompson
Mem. Park

Perrine

FRANJO
RD

23

25

Toll

20

KENDA

Toll

S

874

S

16

18

13

DR

Miami
Metrozoo

EUREKA

**S. Miami
Hts.**

4 mi

4 km

2

2

0

0

absent at night and on weekends. Miamians themselves have hardly had time to get used to the changes that have transformed the central business district out of all recognition. Construction and congestion make it difficult to drive downtown. Parking can be a problem, too. You'll save yourself a lot of trouble if you ride to the centre on Metrorail (all the outlying stations have car parks), transferring to the downtown **Metromover.** This computerised adjunct to the metropolitan transport system loops around the urban core of Miami, with its concentration of high-rise office blocks, shopping arcades, and hotels.

You'll come close to some of the city's lofty new landmarks, including the **First Union Financial Center.** Lunchtime concerts are held in the airy plaza, an urban meeting place designed for Florida living; the outdoor area extends across Biscayne Boulevard into **Claude and Mildred Pepper Bayfront Park.** Cosmopolitan **Flagler Street,** main thoroughfare of the downtown district, is predominantly Latin, and so are the enterprising merchants who offer competitively priced jewellery, clothing, and electronic goods for sale to shoppers from south of the border, enhancing Miami's reputation as the marketplace of the Americas. Among the department stores and small shops of East Flagler stands the **Gusman Center for the Performing Arts,** a 1920s pastiche of Spanish Baroque architecture. Now a venue for concerts and plays, the centre began life as a music hall. Stand-up comics and variety acts invariably played to a full house here, for the Gusman was one of the first air-conditioned buildings in the city; ice used to be packed under the floorboards of the music hall to keep the audience cool.

Miami's love affair with Spanish architecture continues at the **Metro-Dade Cultural Center** (1979), farther on at 101 West Flagler. That master of post-modern architecture, Philip

Johnson, designed the nostalgic stucco and tile structure in collaboration with John Burgee. Three institutions flank a central courtyard: the main branch of the **Miami-Dade Public Library,** largest in the Southeast; the **Miami Museum of Art,** providing gallery space for some superb travelling exhibitions; and the **Historical Museum of Southern Florida,** featuring lots of "hands-on" exhibits (see pages 57-58).

The inauguration of the **James L. Knight International Center** in 1982 set the seal on Miami's reviving fortunes. Situated at the mouth of the Miami River, the centre incorporates a hotel, exhibition hall, meeting rooms, and an indoor sports arena. There is no more historic site in the city than this. Here the Tequesta Indians established a settlement

Miami is a popular embarkation point for luxury cruises to the Caribbean.

some 4,000 years ago, and here Spanish missionaries came to convert them in the 16th century. Here, too, stood the William English house and the barracks of Fort Dallas, founded during the Third Seminole War. Finally, on this spot lived Julia Tuttle, remembered as the "Mother of Miami."

Riverwalk leads from the Knight Center along the north bank of the Miami River, and the promenade out around the bay. Not far away, **José Martí Riverfront Park** offers modern docking facilities and a waterside walkway.

Boat yards, marine suppliers, and industrial installations border the murky Miami River as it winds eastward through the city from the Everglades. Although called a river, it is in fact a saltwater inlet, with no freshwater source of its own.

The Miami Melting Pot

For a long time Miami was as southern as grits and fried chicken. Just about everybody spoke with a drawl in the city they called "Miamah."

After World War II, Northerners and Midwesterners swelled the "Miamee" population. Coming from diverse backgrounds, the newcomers included many Jews of Eastern European origin who brought a taste for borscht and bagels with them.

The arrival of hundreds of thousands of exiles from Cuba in the 1960s and 70s added yet another element to the ethnic equation, as Cuban coffee and black beans took the city by storm.

These days, immigration from Nicaragua, Colombia, Venezuela, Ecuador, and other Central and South American countries is reinforcing the Latin influence, while thousands of Haitians are introducing a Creole flavour into the ethnic stew.

Art Deco at night — neon-illuminated façades create a surreal beachfront skyline.

After a long absence, cargo ships have now returned to the waterway.

At the junction of the Miami River and Biscayne Bay rise the travertine marble towers of the **Miami Convention Center,** an imposing hotel, shopping, office, and condominium complex. In 1895 Julia Tuttle ceded the property to Henry Flagler, who built his luxury hotel, the Royal Palm, on this spot. The opulent Hotel Inter-Continental continues that grand tradition.

The older downtown hostelries overlook **Biscayne Boulevard,** with its central island of palms. This sweeping thoroughfare is the scene of the Miami Grand Prix, contested by champions of the motor-racing world. The boulevard also plays host to the King Orange Jamboree Parade, a New Year's Eve event since 1936.

Across the way, the green expanse of **Bayfront Park** edges Biscayne Bay. At one time motorists used to speed by with little more than a glance at the palms and shrubbery, or at the John F. Kennedy Torch of Friendship, a symbol of goodwill between the United States and its neighbours to the south.

That was before the **Bayside Market Place** started building on 20 acres of parkland. Today, Bayside's complex of boutiques, restaurants, and food courts are busy day and night. Concerts are frequently held at the dockside, from which many day sightseeing vessels depart. A variety of cruises is offered, from weekend jaunts to the nearby Bahamas to voyages of a week or more into the Caribbean.

Building on Sand

A dozen artificial isles grace Biscayne Bay: the Venetian Islands, the Sunset group, and Palm, Star, and Hibiscus islands. The by-product of channel dredging operations, these geometric strips of land provide the maximum of waterfront footage.

Carl Fisher refined the dredging procedure on Miami Beach (which is itself three-quarters fill). Beginning in 1913, his machines scooped up material from the bay bottom, including decaying animal and vegetable matter, and turned it into dikes. The stench was terrific, but Fisher discovered that the odour disappeared as the soupy material solidified. Rich, black soil could then be spread over the sand, and trees planted to retain the land.

The islands in the bay have been secluded retreats for personalities as diverse as Howard Hughes and Al Capone. The gangster acquired his grand, Spanish-style house at 93 Palm Island in 1928, shortly before the St. Valentine's Day Massacre. Indicted for income-tax evasion several years later, Capone was forced to abandon the palm trees for prison. He returned to Miami on his release in 1939, and lived here until he died, eight years later, of syphilis.

A causeway leads across the water to the Dodge Island premises of the **Port of Miami,** "Cruise Capital of the World." Several million passengers a year set sail from Miami. On weekends, as many as eight ocean-going liners can be seen lying at anchor in the port.

Farther up the boulevard stands **Freedom Tower**—a relic of the 1920s modelled after the Giralda tower in Seville, Spain. Built for the *Miami Daily News*, the 17-storey edifice acquired its present name during the Cuban exodus, when the Refugee Center had headquarters in the tower.

Beyond Bicentennial Park, you pass the entrance to scenic **MacArthur Causeway,** which cuts across Watson Island on its way to Miami Beach. There's a great **view** of the port from the island. On any given day, as well as ocean-going liners, gigantic tankers lie at anchor there, dwarfing the never-ending parade of pleasure craft.

Back on the mainland itself, the offices of the *Miami Herald* extend along the bayfront from the MacArthur Causeway to the **Venetian Causeway,** in sight of the man-made islands of the Venetian chain. Just opposite, the concrete bulk of **Plaza Venetia** reflects in the mirror of the bay. This self-contained skyscraper block boasts its own marina, restaurants, and shops.

A skywalk connects the Marriott Hotel at Plaza Venetia to **Omni International** in Biscayne Boulevard. A suburban-style shopping mall transplanted to the city centre, Omni has department stores, chain concerns, and fast-food outlets, as well as cinemas, child-care facilities—and a luxury hotel for good measure.

The northern stretch of Biscayne Boulevard, developed for commerce during the Depression, retains many low-rise structures from the 1930s. They alternate with purpose-built office blocks, such as the blue-and-white tiled headquarters of Bacardi International, the rum company. Stop off at the **Bacardi Art Gallery** (at 2000 Biscayne Boulevard), where a changing succession of contemporary art exhibitions attracts a discerning public on weekdays.

Miami's financial district lies south of the Miami River in the area of **Brickell Avenue.** It is known as "the Wall Street of the South"—and that is no exaggeration. In recent years, nearly 100 international banks specializing in foreign transactions have opened offices here. While New York trades with Europe, an ocean away, and Los Angeles deals with the distant Far East, Miami has an expanding market with Latin America right at its doorstep.

South of Brickell, the graceful mansions of an earlier era share the coastline with such luxury high-rise condominiums as the Atlantis, Imperial, and Palace. If the new Miami has a symbol, it is the blue rectangle of the **Atlantis,** with its 12th-storey sky court featuring a free-form jacuzzi, full-grown palm tree, and high-tech stairway to the stars. The critics call it "Beach Blanket Bauhaus."

Little Havana

For many Americans, Little Havana is as foreign as Paris or Rome. Here in the Cuban enclave, the Latinisation of Miami is complete. Little Havana covers a 9 sq km (3½-square-mile) section of the city, bounded roughly by West Flagler Street and Coral Way, I-95 and 37th Avenue.

Although tourists are undoubtedly drawn to the neighbourhood, it's not really a tourist attraction so much as a vital centre of Hispanic life. Anglos and Cubans alike patronise the tempting fruit stands, bakeries, and supermarkets, and the shops selling records, clothing, and shoes. Spanish-language cinemas, bilingual schools, and tailors all have premises in this lively community of 200,000 residents.

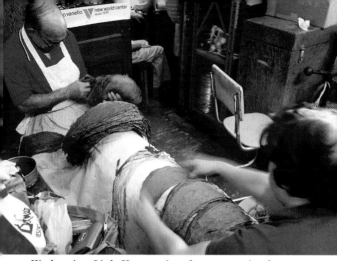

Workers in a Little Havana cigar factory practice the art of rolling cigars by hand.

The business district centres on S.W. 8th Street, better known as **Calle Ocho**—a one-way thoroughfare that runs from west to east, linking Coral Gables to the downtown district. After a coffee at one of the streetside counters, stop to watch the chess and domino games in **Antonio Maceo Park,** at the crossing of 14th Avenue. Cuban women may have entered the workforce, but they have yet to penetrate this male preserve filled with cigar smoke and the clicking sound of the playing pieces.

On the opposite side of the street, a mural depicts the patron saint of Cuba, the *Virgen de la Caridad* (Our Lady of Charity). In the 17th century, she appeared to three mariners from Cuba in a vision, saving them from shipwreck—or so the story goes.

 **Coconut Grove**

Augustus St. Gaudens and Alexander Graham Bell had homes in the Grove, and American writers James Whitcomb Riley, Robert Frost, and Tennessee Williams did a lot of work here. Hip in the 1960s, trendy in the 1980s, the freewheeling Grove is Miami's bohemia.

Coconut Grove embraces the bayfront from S.W. 32nd Road to Battersea Road, extending inland to U.S. 1 and Le Jeune Road. Absorbed by an expanding Miami in 1925, the Grove is an urban village within the city limits. People from all over converge on the village centre, where dozens of small shops offer clothing, jewellery, pottery, and ethnic items.

A stately old structure presides over the bayfront: **Vizcaya Museum and Garden,** the Italian-Renaissance-style mansion completed in 1916 for James Deering, scion of the International Harvester family. Purchased by Dade County in 1952, the house, with its fabulous furnishings, is open to the public daily (see page 55).

Because of its outdoor lifestyle, the Grove hosts a number of festivals, jamborees, and sporting events throughout the year. In February, for example, there's the three-day **Coconut Grove Arts Festival,** with more than 300 visual and performing artists participating. In June, Grand Avenue reverberates to the sounds of the **Goombay Festival,** celebrating the Bahamian heritage of Miami's first black settlers.

Weekends and evenings the traffic can be chaotic, as crowds jam the sidewalk cafés and garden restaurants along **Main Highway, Commodore Plaza,** and **McFarlane Road** in the heart of the Grove. Choose a table early or reserve in advance—it's standing room only here after dark. Even at the best of times driving can be difficult in Coconut Grove. You'll see more if you explore the area by bike or on foot.

A showcase for good theatre, the **Coconut Grove Play-house** stands at the crossing of Main Highway and Charles Avenue, where Dade County's first African-American settle-ment grew up. A State Historic Site lies directly opposite— **The Barnacle,** first home on the bay (see pages 66).

It's a short walk under the banyans to **Plymouth Congre-gational Church,** just off Main Highway, in Devon Road. A

Sidewalk cafés are a mainstay at Coconut Grove, a perennial center of culture in Miami.

On the Key Biscayne, bayfront sea and sky converge in a sunset panorama.

Grove landmark since 1917, the vine-clad coral-rock edifice looks positively timeworn. In the grounds stands the Grove's original schoolhouse, a one-room wood-frame affair knocked together with timber salvaged from shipwrecks. Main Highway runs into McFarlane Road, which leads past grassy Peacock Park to the bay. A plaque in the park marks the location of Peacock Inn, Dade County's first hotel, which was opened in 1882.

Dinner Key Marina, packed with hundreds of sailing boats, is a picturesque spot. In the old days picnic parties used to row out from the harbour for lunch or dinner, which accounts for the name. Site of a U.S. naval air base during World Wars I and II, Dinner Key was also home to the flying clippers of Pan American Airways in the 1930s. Right on the bay, the Art-Deco terminal building now serves as Miami's City Hall, while the old hangars serve as the Coconut Grove Exhibition Center, scene of the annual boat, dog, and home shows.

Joggers, roller bladers, and fitness fanatics are thick on the ground at **David Kennedy Park,** which occupies an attractively landscaped sweep of bayfront. Across South Bay Shore Drive, the five-star Grand Bay and the Doubletree Hotel overlook the water, while the select Mayfair House stands above Coconut Grove's enclosed Mall, **Mayfair-in-the-Grove.**

Coral Gables

Winding streets, sweeping lawns, and some gracious colonial- and Mediterranean-style homes make the affluent Gables a model of suburbia. Citizens jog, cycle, and play golf and tennis in a setting of shade trees and ornamental fountains 10 km (six miles) from downtown. Founded in 1925, the "City Beautiful" was America's first planned community.

Discreet signs bearing the words "Coral Gables Self-Guided Tour" direct visitors to points of interest around the town. Ask for a map of the route in City Hall, the colonnaded building constructed in 1928 at the crossing of Le Jeune Road, Biltmore Way, Coral Way, and Miracle Mile. Miraculous mainly in name, the Mile is the principal shopping street of Coral Gables.

Follow Coral Way to **Coral Gables House,** childhood home of Gables developer George Merrick. The city takes its name from this coral-rock residence of 1906, which has a gabled roof of red barrel tiles (see page 68).

A few streets away at **Venetian Pool,** in DeSoto Boulevard, arched footbridges and arcaded buildings reflect in the waters of an artificial lagoon. Originally a quarry for the coral rock used in early Gables construction, the pool was transformed from eyesore to beauty spot by Merrick. During the boom, swimming competitions featuring Johnny Weissmuller brought the crowds out to Coral Gables. People have

The South Pacific meets the Adriatic at the ornate Venetian Pool.

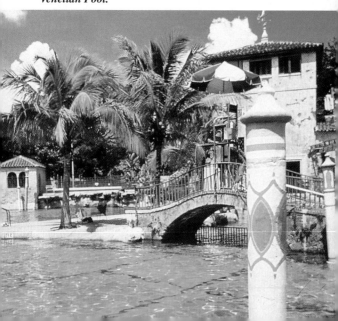

been coming ever since, attracted by "the world's most beautiful swimming hole."

The most prominent building around, the towering **Biltmore Hotel** (Anastasia Avenue) was the last word in luxury accommodation and resort facilities during its prewar heyday. Guests enjoyed the golf courses, polo fields, and tennis courts on the premises. And when the charms of America's largest hotel swimming pool palled, there was always the private beach on the bayfront, reached by gondola via an artificial waterway. Like Freedom Tower on Biscayne Boulevard, the hotel was modelled after Seville's Giralda Tower; it has been restored to its former glory.

From modest beginnings in the 1920s, the **University of Miami** (off U.S. 1) has developed into a leading centre of learning, known internationally for its Institute of Marine and Atmospheric Science. The **Lowe Art Museum** in the university grounds presents some excellent temporary exhibitions, in addition to possessing a good study collection of Renaissance and Baroque paintings (see page 56).

South along the bayfront, Coral Gables encompasses **Matheson Hammock,** 227 hectares (560 acres) of mangroves, live oaks, nature trails, picnic areas, boat docks, and beaches. Neighbouring **Fairchild Tropical Garden,** an Eden of orchids, ferns, and palms, is one of the most popular horticultural attractions in the United States (see pages 59).

THE BEACHES

The Miami oceanfront has always been a great recreational asset, attractive to tourists and residents alike. In the old days, ferryboats provided access to the sea. Now a series of causeways spans Biscayne Bay, connecting the mainland to the Beaches.

 **Miami Beach**

For a lot of people, Miami means the Beach—the resort island that is America's most durable winter playground. The famous oceanfront hotels stretch for 11 km (seven miles) from Government Cut to 87th Street. They include streamlined survivors from the 1930s and peerless monuments of '50s kitsch. For a time after World War II, more luxury hotels were constructed in Miami Beach than in the rest of the world combined. The appeal of Miami Beach waned a bit in the 1970s and 1980s as sun worshippers headed instead to the Caribbean, but now business is picking up again as Europeans and a younger crowd frequent the Beach.

MacArthur Causeway enters the island at 5th Street, near the expanded **Miami Beach Marina.** Fishing charters operate from this public facility, which incorporates nautical shops, a waterfront restaurant, and an outdoor café. The neighbourhood is the oldest on the Beach. Redevelopment has claimed most of the early landmarks, although **Joe's Stone Crab Restaurant** in Biscayne Street still stands its ground. A Miami Beach institution since 1913, Joe's narrowly escaped demolition when buildings in the area were razed to make way for South Pointe, a hotel, office, and condominium complex. **South Pointe Park,** a new centre of leisure and recreation, covers the southernmost tip of Miami Beach.

North of 6th Street, in **South Beach,** the **Art Deco District** offers architecture—and more. Preservationists involved in the restoration of this historic area invite you to return to the tropical '30s. The setting is compelling: 800 buildings in distinctive Art-Deco style line the streets of a zone stretching up to 23rd Street. The concentration of Art-Deco architecture is the greatest in the world, and buildings sport sunbursts, waves, palm trees, and flamingoes: fantasy meets futurism on Miami Beach.

You can join a **walking tour** of the district, organised by the Miami Design Preservation League, on Thursday evenings and Saturday mornings. The starting point is league headquarters, the **Art Deco District Welcome Center** at 1001 Ocean Drive. You can also rent audiotapes for a self-guided tour and load up on printed information; a gift shop sells memorabilia.

Now known as SoBe, this South Beach district is the hottest tourist destination in South Florida. A babble of tongues is heard on **Ocean Drive** as visitors from all over

Miami Beach Moderne: Art Deco with a Southern accent on Washington Avenue.

the world flock to its sidewalk cafés, night spots, and Art-Deco hotels. Fashion photographers delight in the pastel-coloured backdrop the district provides. Get up early in the morning and you'll see models and photographers at work catching the young sun against the Art-Deco buildings.

Away from the sands, the world of Art Deco also embraces commercial **Washington Avenue,** a mosaic of markets. Posting a letter is less of a chore in the Art Moderne surroundings of the Miami Beach Post Office at number 1300, while farther up the street a sizable congregation worships beneath the Middle-Eastern domes of Temple Emanu-El, a late Art-Deco monument of 1947. The presence of a couple of Cuban restaurants and food shops along Washington highlights the changing ethnic character of the area. The Wolfsonian Foundation Gallery at 1001 Washington Avenue houses a fascinating collection of 20th-century memorabilia and modern design; the collections are nicely set off by the surroundings, a 1927 building.

True to its name, **Espanola Way** recreates the atmosphere of a Spanish village. Constructed before the craze for streamlined architecture swept Miami Beach, this ensemble of Mediterranean-Revival buildings teems with tourists at night, when the street becomes a pedestrian-only passage. At the far end of Espanola, you come to expansive **Flamingo Park,** the haunt of tennis players day and night.

Artists and craftsmen are also moving into **Lincoln Road Mall,** the street once called the "Fifth Avenue of the South." Open-air trams still circulate along the pedestrian thoroughfare, with its low-rise Art-Deco shop fronts, but most of the old glamour is gone.

Where the marquees match the cars: a study in the pinks and pastels of Miami Beach.

Housed in an elegant 1930s structure of coral rock, the **Bass Museum** in Park Avenue is a bastion of culture on the Beach. In addition to having an eclectic permanent collection, the museum organises some timely exhibitions (see pages 57). Jazz concerts on Sundays bring out the devotees of Art-Deco.

On the periphery of the Art Deco District is that busy facility, the **Miami Beach Convention Center,** and the 3,000-seat **Jackie Gleason Theater of the Performing Arts.** A lot of people prefer to approach the Beach just west of here, via the Venetian Causeway and Dade Boulevard.

The rambling **Miami Beach Boardwalk** begins at 21st Street and runs out along the water, behind the big hotels, as far as 46th. The rustic wooden walkway made an immediate hit when it opened in 1984. Covered pavilions provide a place to sit and contemplate the panorama of sea and sky. "No Skating, No Dogs," warn the signs. The beach itself is something of a phenomenon: 90 metres (300 feet) wide, it stretches to infinity.

Time was when at least one new luxury hotel a year opened in the part of Collins Avenue known as **hotel row.** Now the street is built up all the way to Sunny Isles. There's the Seville, the Sans Souci, the Versailles, the Barcelona ... the sweep of concrete seems inevitable, as much a part of the landscape as Indian Creek or the ink-blue Atlantic.

Revamped during the '80s, the fabulous **Fontainebleau Hilton** continues to lord it over them all. People wander in for a look at the free-form pool with its grottoes and cascades—the slick new symbol of a reviving Miami Beach. For nostalgia seekers, the Boom Boom Room and Poodle Lounge are still going strong.

Amidst all this glitter are two "serious" landmarks of note: a sobering **Holocaust Memorial** in the 1900 block of Meridian Avenue, and the recently expanded **Bass Museum of Art,** with a commendable collection of European paintings (including works by Rubens and Dürer) at 2121 Park Avenue.

Condominiums proliferate in the northern reaches of Collins, a mecca for retired New Yorkers. Yachts tie up along Indian Creek, and there are some great golfing greens in the area, like the municipal Normandy Shores course on **Normandy Isle.** The 79th Street Causeway provides a direct link to the mainland by way of North Bay Village.

Key Biscayne

So many Miamians converge on this "Island Paradise" at weekends that the city had to erect a 26-metre (85-foot) bridge to accommodate all the traffic. Residents are resigned to the crowds. You can't keep people out of paradise.

English explorer John Cabot sighted Key Biscayne in 1497. Juan Ponce de León followed him here in 1513. The Spaniard called the island *Santa Marta*, but the Indian name survived: "Biscayne" is a corruption of *Bischiyano,* "The Favourite Path of the Rising Moon." A military base during the Second Seminole War, Key Biscayne later became the resort of wreckers and then of hunters and fishermen.

A few escapists built homes on the island in the early years of the century, but development came only with the opening of Rickenbacker Causeway in 1947. Thanks to extensive parkland at the north and south of the island, Key Biscayne retains an aspect of natural beauty rare in metropolitan Miami.

It's a long, leisurely ride across the water to the island. Early in the day, the causeway beaches fill up with windsurfers and waterskiers. As you cross the causeway, be sure to spare a glance for Miami's evolving skyline, visible in the middle distance; you can always pull off the road for a lingering look on the return journey.

Flipper the dolphin and Lolita the killer whale cavort for the crowds at the **Miami Seaquarium,** just opposite. The shows are continuous, so no matter when you arrive you'll be on time for one of them (see page 63). Alongside the Seaquarium stands the University of Miami's Institute of Marine Science. The proximity of the two institutions is more than coincidental, for they cooperate in the study of underwater life.

Another stretch of causeway brings you to Key Biscayne itself. Dozens of sailing boats lie at anchor in **Crandon Marina,** painting the bay waters red, yellow, and blue. Tufted clouds overhead echo the convolutions of the mangroves. Pelicans and gulls perch on the piers.

On the ocean side of the island, the 4 km (2½-mile) public beach of **Crandon Park** attracts more than a million people a year, from swimmers and sunbathers to Frisbee players. Barefoot joggers head south along the beach past the big hotels and condominium blocks to historic Cape Florida, also accessible by bikeway and road. And there's always a procession of walkers just taking it easy.

Crandon Boulevard leads through the unassuming town centre to the **Bill Baggs Cape Florida State Recreation Area,** 165 hectares (406 acres) covering the southern tip of the island. Here the waters of the Atlantic meet those of Biscayne Bay. Closed for a year after Hurricane Andrew devastated it,

the park was virtually denuded of trees, but is slowly regaining its beauty.

At weekends and on public holidays Cape Florida's beach can get so crowded that the entrance gates have to be closed early in the afternoon. But most of the time Cape Florida is the peaceful haunt of sea birds. In the nesting season, ponderous turtles struggle across the sand to lay their eggs. The old **Cape Florida Lighthouse** (see page 67) dominates the southern

Palm trees are ubiquitous throughout the greater Miami area.

beach front. Several times a day, park rangers guide visitors around the site. Go for a swim and come back for a fascinating tour of inspection.

Leaving the park, you can turn off towards **Hurricane Harbor,** on the bay, for a quick spin through former president Richard Nixon's old neighbourhood. But don't look for the former Winter White House—it has long since been knocked down.

North to the Beach Communities

Eight streets long, the friendly village of **Surfside** is especially popular with French Canadians—so popular that the community organises a "Salute to Canada" festival every year in late February or early March. Families of all nationalities are attracted by Surfside's pleasant beach, reasonable hotel rates, and informal air.

The desirable resort community of **Bal Harbour** lies farther north along Collins. (It's also accessible from the North Miami mainland by Broad Causeway.) Deluxe hotels crowd the oceanfront, within hailing distance of **Bal Harbour Shops,** a luxury mall in an attractive garden setting of orange trees, palms, and shrubs. Ranged over two landscaped levels. Neiman Marcus, Bonwit Teller, and Saks Fifth Avenue join forces with some of the best-known names in international fashion—Gucci, Mark Cross, Charles Jourdan, Cartier, Yves Saint-Laurent, and Guy Laroche, to list just a few. In the car park, uniformed guards in pith helmets keep a watchful eye on all the Mercedes and Rolls-Royces.

Beyond Bal Harbour, Collins crosses **Haulover Beach Park,** a popular Metro-Dade facility. There's swimming along a two-mile stretch of sand (ocean currents can be strong; the northern portion of the beach is popular with nude sunbathers), fishing from a 1,100-foot pier, as well as golf, tennis, and deep-sea fishing by charter craft hired from the Haulover marina. You can also board an excursion boat for a tour of Biscayne Bay and other points of interest in Greater Miami.

Collins leads on to **Sunny Isles,** famous in the 1960s as a magnet for singles and swingers, but more sedate these days. (The Sunny Isles Causeway runs directly from North Miami Beach —on the mainland, despite the name—to the resort.) Fishermen frequent the pier at the junction of the causeway and Collins, a kaleidoscope of coffee shops, delicatessens, restaurants, bars, clubs, and motels.

In fact, **Motel Row** stretches for 3 km (2 miles) or so along the ocean side of the street. The theme motels are architectural classics of the pop era: the Tahiti has a Polynesian motif; the Sahara sports stucco camels.

MUSEUMS

Vizcaya Museum and Gardens, at 3251 South Miami Avenue, Tel. (305) 250-9133; daily, 9:30 A.M.–4:30 P.M., gardens until 5:30 P.M.; fee. The Italian-Renaissance-style mansion— magnificent former residence of tractor millionaire James Deering—incorporates some precious architectural elements: pink marble gateways from the Palazzo Bevilacqua in Verona, a carved stucco ceiling from the Palazzo Rossi in Venice, and an Adam mantelpiece from Rathfarnham Castle in Dublin.

Deering personally acquired it all. Not the typical captain of industry but a jet-setter equally at home in France and the United States, he had an exquisite and highly developed sense of style. Deering's health was already failing when the house reached completion in 1916. Eight short years were left to him to enjoy his creation.

Dade County purchased the estate and 30 acres of hammock in 1952. The Deering heirs contributed the original furnishings, including Ferrara tapestries from the collection of Duke Ercole II, a 16th-century trestle table with a Farnese provenance, and a handsome Neapolitan bed that belonged to Lady Hamilton, paramour of Lord Nelson, England's great admiral.

Volunteer guides conduct tours of the house at frequent intervals throughout the day. Restoration work permitting, you'll see every nook and cranny, from the imposing Renaissance Hall to the tiny Rococo telephone room and wood-panelled lift — Neo-Classical tour-de-force of the Otis Elevator Company.

Lush formal **gardens** descend from the house to the bay. Like the hill gardens of Italy, they contain statuary, fountains, hidden grottoes, and a casino, or place of retreat. Deering commissioned Gaston Lachaise to carve the birds on the Peacock Bridge, and he entrusted the figures on the stone barge (a breakwater) to the skills of the leading sculptor of the day, A. Stirling Calder, father of the more famous Alexander. Across South Miami Avenue, the Superintendent's House on the farm that once supplied Vizcaya with poultry, fruit, and vegetables has been renovated to display the **Claire Mendel Collection** (50 S.W. 32nd Road) of 15th- to 19th-century painting and sculpture (open weekends only). The works of art were donated to Vizcaya by a citizen of Miami Beach.

Miami Art Museum, in the Metro-Dade Cultural Center at 101 West Flagler Street; Tel. (305) 375-1700; Tuesday–Friday, 10:00 A.M.–5:00 P.M., weekends, noon–5:00 P.M.; fee. Check the local newspapers for details of travelling exhibitions periodically on view.

University of Miami's Lowe Art Museum, off U.S. 1 at 1301 Stanford Drive in the Gables, Tel. (305) 284-3535; Tuesday–Saturday, 10:00 A.M.–5:00 P.M., Sunday, noon–5:00 P.M.; fee. In addition to special shows and lectures, the Lowe also houses the Kress Collection of Renaissance and

Baroque art, an important cultural resource for Miami, with works by Lippo Vanni, Andrea della Robbia, Lucas Cranach the Elder, and others. Miami is one of U.S. cities to benefit from the philanthropy of Samuel H. Kress, founder of the Kress chain of five-and-dime stores.

The Cuban Museum of the Americas, 1300 S.W. 12th Avenue, Tel. (305) 858-8006; Tuesday–Friday, noon–6:00 P.M.; fee. Situated in a quiet residential neighbourhood of Little Havana, this museum organises exhibitions and events with a Latin accent, features members of the Cuban vanguard in exile, including the "Miami Generation" of artists who came of age in the United States. This is one of the most vital institutions in Miami, dedicated to preserving Cuba's cultural traditions.

The Bass Museum of Art, 2121 Park Avenue, Tel. (305) 673-7530; Tuesday–Saturday, 10:00 A.M.–5:00 P.M., Sunday, 1:00 P.M.–5:00 P.M., closed second and fourth Wednesday of each month; fee. This museum brings some stimulating travelling exhibitions to Miami Beach. In 1964, Austrian-born entrepreneur John Bass and his wife, Johanna, presented most of the works of art on permanent display. Bass bought what he liked: European paintings, sculpture, Asian bronzes, and ecclesiastical vestments. Docents, or volunteer guides, will point out the highlights.

The Historical Museum of Southern Florida has premises downtown in the Metro-Dade Cultural Center, 101 West Flagler Street, Tel. (305) 375-2665; Monday–Saturday, 10:00 A.M.–5:00 P.M. (Thursday until 9:00 P.M.), Sunday, noon–5:00 P.M.; fee. Displays recall 10,000 years of history in the area, as well as the geological events that shaped the land. The outstanding single exhibit is a rare, double-elephant folio of Audubon's *Birds of America,* valued at more than $1 million. Tequesta artefacts take pride of place in the American Indian section, one of the largest in the United

States. Audiovisual presentations dramatise episodes from the more recent past—19th-century anthropologist Clay MacCauley's encounter with the Miccosukee tribe and Ralph Middleton Munroe's experiences as a Coconut Grove pioneer. The Coral Gables Trolley will transport you back to the 1920s, when everybody in Miami had land fever. But the most haunting relics are those of yesterday, a somewhat shabby Mercury space capsule and a Haitian refugee boat that somehow made it to shore in 1979.

Holocaust Memorial, 1933-1945 Meridian Avenue, Tel. (305) 538-1663, daily 9:00 A.M.–9:00 P.M.; free. At the centre of the memorial—not so much a museum as a poignant reminder of man's inhumanity to man—a gigantic bronze arm and hand stretches toward the sky. Photographs and a Memorial Wall pay tribute to Jewish victims of Nazi terror. Encircling the monument, the walls of a tunnel-like passage show images of the Nazi death camps.

ATTRACTIONS

You may not have time for all of them, but you'll certainly want to take in a few. Make your choice from the list below.

Biscayne National Park, Homestead; write or telephone for information and reservations: P.O. Box 1369, Homestead, Florida, Tel. (305) 230-1144. Or contact the Biscayne Aqua-Center, Tel. (305) 230-1100. This marine preserve covers 175,000 acres of water and land in Biscayne Bay, including Elliot Key and 23 attendant islets. Boat tours open up the underwater world, a sanctuary for sea creatures large and small, including manatees, turtles, stone crabs, spiny lobsters, and shrimps. Park rangers are on hand to provide commentaries and answer questions.

Butterfly World, Tradewinds Park, 3600 W. Sample Road, Coconut Creek, Tel. (954) 977-4400; Monday–Saturday,

9:00 A.M.–5:00 P.M., Sunday 1:00 P.M.–5:00 P.M.; fee. No less colourful or exotic than sea creatures are the butterflies and moths that flutter freely through the three giant aviaries of Butterfly World. A tropical rain forest has been screened in to provide a suitable habitat for more than 150 species. You can stroll through the vine walk and gardens, and see some unusual insects in the "Museum-Insectarium."

Fairchild Tropical Garden, 10901 Old Cutler Road, Coral Gables; Tel. (305) 667-1651; daily, 9:30 A.M.–4:30 P.M.; fee. Exotic plants, trees and flowers from around the world thrive in this bayside botanical showplace. There are hundreds of varieties of palms alone, including the African oil palm, the South American honey palm, the smooth-trunked Bailey palm, and the petticoat palm, skirted with fronds. In

Not just for the birds — other flora and fauna native to Florida are also represented at Parrot Jungle.

a glade of their own grow the palm-like cycads, plants that flourished during the Cretaceous Period, when dinosaurs stalked the earth. Water cascades through the Rare Plant House, steamy shelter for orchids, bromeliads, and a profusion of ferns, while sprinklers make up for any shortage of water in the rain forest. Go for a circuit of the garden by tram, or join a guided walking tour for more leisurely exploration.

Gold Coast Railroad Museum, S.W. 152nd Street and S.W. 124th Avenue; Tel. (305) 253-0063; daily, 11:00 A.M.–3:00 P.M. (weekends until 4:00 P.M.); fee. You'll see some historic rolling stock here, including the glass-domed observation car of the Chicago-to-San-Francisco *California Zephyr* and the *Ferdinand Magellan*, one-time private Pullman car of the President of the United States. Custom-fitted with steel armour plating, bulletproof glass, and two escape hatches, the *Magellan* has a special brass-railed platform at the rear from which the head of state could declaim. On weekends, the museum takes tourists for a ride on a vintage train pulled by an old Seaboard steam locomotive.

☛ **Hialeah Park Race Course,** 2200 E. 4th Avenue, Hialeah; Tel. (305) 885-8000. The racehorses pound the oval at Hialeah only two months a year, either in January and February or March and April. The rest of the time, the track opens its gates daily to tourists. You can visit the grand French-style clubhouse, formal gardens, paddock area, and backstretch with stables for 1,500 thoroughbreds. Hialeah's famous pink flamingoes fly over the infield every afternoon. Born at the track, the birds never stray far from their native turf. Although children under the age of 18 aren't allowed to attend race meetings, they are welcome to breakfast in the

At Metrozoo, a white tiger lounges regally while waiting for his next meal.

clubhouse at weekends, when a commentator is on hand to talk about the horses as they exercise.

Ichimura Japanese Garden, Watson Island, just off MacArthur Causeway. This tranquil garden, donated to the city of Miami by Japanese industrialist Kiyoshi Ichimura in 1961, includes a 300-year-old stone lantern, rock gardens, and a giant statue of Hotei, the smiling Japanese god of prosperity.

Metrozoo, 12400 Coral Reef Drive, Tel. (305) 251-0400; daily 9:00 A.M.–5:30 P.M.; fee. This cageless facility is one of the most progressive zoos in the world. Animals compatible with the South Florida climate live in surroundings that closely approximate their natural habitat. White Bengal tigers prowl around a replica of a 13th-century shrine at Angkor Wat, and African grazing animals lope across a miniature facsimile of the Serengeti Plain.

"Wings of Asia," Metrozoo's remarkable .5-hectare (1½-acre) free-flight aviary, was destroyed by Hurricane Andrew; it is to be rebuilt.

Miami Museum of Science and Space Transit Planetarium, 3280 South Miami Avenue; Tel. (305) 854-4247; daily, 10:00 A.M.–6:00 P.M.; fee. The "hands-on" exhibits here show various phenomena of nature in action, from the refraction of light to the generation of electricity. Popular with school groups, the museum presents slide shows, films, and live demonstrations, including glass-blowing and dissections. Ask for an "explainer" to take you round. At the **Southern Cross Astronomical Observatory,** you can behold the Miami moon through a 14-inch Celestron telescope or a Clark antique of 1900. The observatory is open free of charge in the evening at weekends and on Sunday afternoons, when the sun is under scrutiny. In the Space Transit Planetarium, multi-media shows alternate with astronomy programmes and laser spectaculars (lights and rock music).

Miami Seaquarium, Rickenbacker Causeway; Tel. (305) 361-5705; daily, 9:30 A.M.–6:00 P.M.; fee. Don't miss film-star Flipper in a live appearance. The dolphin frolics with some fishy friends on the original set of the Flipper television show preserved for posterity at the Seaquarium. Lolita, the lovable killer whale, goes through her paces in the Whale Bowl, while Salty the sea lion takes centre stage in a marine magic show. For their part, the man-eaters in the shark channel do what comes naturally as they lunge—most convincingly—for bloody hunks of fish flesh. A sign nearby warns, "Danger! Hungry Live Sharks." And so they are! You'll want to look in on the manatees, or sea cows, including Lorelei, the first to be conceived and born in captivity (1975). That leaves thousands of

Killer whales and other creatures of the sea perform daily at Seaquarium.

species more to discover—the denizens of the Reef Aquarium and some two dozen wall tanks in the Main Aquarium.

Miami Youth Museum, 3301 Coral Way, Tel. (305) 446-4386; Monday–Friday, 10:00 A.M.–5:00 P.M., Saturday–Sunday, 11:00 A.M.–6:00 P.M.; fee. (Call first—the Youth Museum is planning to relocate to Coconut Grove.) The museum's "Kidscape" offers younger members of the family an opportunity to explore a mini-neighbourhood, complete with a fire station, supermarket, and dental office. Hands-on cultural and daily-life displays provide educational fun designed to encourage creativity.

Monkey Jungle, 14805 Hinlin Mill Drive, Tel. (305) 253-1611; daily, 9:30 A.M.–5:00 P.M.; fee. Some 500 primates make their home in the treetops and jungle paths of this commercial

At Parrot Jungle, some birds just stand around, while others proudly perform for their supper.

attraction. The cages here are for the visitors; the orangutans, gorillas, baboons, gibbons, and others wander at will. Shows take place several times a day. Trained chimps look cute for the tourists' cameras in the Monkey Theatre, while Java monkeys and crab-eating macaques ("skin-diving wild monkeys") demonstrate their acrobatic underwater skills in the Monkey Swimming Pool. Watch your fingers; these monkeys can bite.

Parrot Jungle, 11000 S.W. 57th Avenue; Tel. (305) 666-7834; daily, 9:30 A.M.–6:00 P.M.; fee. (Call first—Parrot Jungle is planning to relocate in a new facility on Watson Island.) Articulate and numerate, the birds at the Parrot Jungle sing, laugh, and cry, can count forwards and backwards, and add and subtract. Watch them perform in daily shows repeated every hour and a half. Afterwards you can wander through 12 hectares (29 acres) of hammock where more birds fly free. A total of 74 different species are on show—1,200 birds in all. Aviaries house some of the more exotic, like the great billed parrot from the Molucca Islands, the Patagonian conure, and the green Amazon parrot. The macaws, on the giant perches by the entrance, provide the ultimate photo opportunity. Let them pose in pairs on your arms and shoulders for Miami's classic tourist shot.

John Pennekamp Coral Reef State Park, U.S. 1, Key Largo; Tel. (305) 451-1202: daily, 8:00 A.M.–sunset; fee. Named in honour of John Pennekamp, a *Miami Herald* reporter who championed the preservation of South Florida's coral reef, this underwater preserve lies to the south of Biscayne National Park. Glass-bottom and snorkel boats ferry visitors 10 km (6 miles) out to Molasses Reef for a fascinating look below water.

Redland Fruit and Spice Park, 24801 Redland Road, Homestead; Tel: (305) 247-5927; daily, 10:00 A.M.–5:00 P.M.; fee. At this 20-acre "living-plant museum" in Homestead, about 30 miles south of Miami, you can see all manner of exotic fruits, nuts, herbs, and spices growing. The park has more than 500 varieties.

HISTORIC SITES

Progress and hurricanes have erased much of Miami's past, but a few monuments remain from that not-so-distant time before the railway, when Indians and alligators had the run of the place.

Barnacle State Historic Site, 3485 Main Highway, Coconut Grove; Tel. (305) 448-9445; Friday–Sunday, 9:00 A.M.–4:00 P.M.; fee. On a stretch of shoreline redeveloped with condominiums, the Barnacle, set in a luxuriant garden, survives from the era of the bay. Naval architect Ralph Middleton Munroe built the wood-frame structure in 1891, using timber salvaged from shipwrecks. Later, when his family outgrew the place, Munroe simply jacked the structure up and added a second floor underneath. Electricity was supplied in 1913, and plumbing was installed in the 1920s. Occupied by the Munroes until 1973, the house has been returned to its original appearance.

Photographs of old Dade County taken by Ralph Munroe decorate the sitting room, filled with dark wooden furniture and a collection of books. Upstairs, the dining room has built-in cabinets modelled on those of a yacht, and the breezy bedrooms display articles of clothing and memorabilia. In the open attic at the top of the house you'll see an early "air conditioner" —a skylight with a series of windows that can be opened and closed in order to create suction and drive out hot air.

Down by the bay you can see Ralph Munroe's boathouse and the shallow-draught *Micco,* designed by Munroe the same year as the house. The craft broke records in 1892 when it sailed to New Jersey in six days.

Cape Florida Lighthouse, Bill Baggs State Recreation Area, Key Biscayne. By local standards, this structure of 1825 is more than venerable. Indians attacked the lighthouse during the Second Seminole War. Damaged in the skirmish, the tower was later raised to a height of 29 metres (95 feet). At the beginning of the Civil War, supporters of the Confederacy destroyed the lantern. It was restored, used until 1878,

Hurricane Watch

A hurricane is a doughnut-shaped vortex of wind that whirls around a calm centre, or "eye," at a speed of 120 km (75 miles) an hour or more. Measuring anything from 60 to several hundred miles in diameter, it travels at about 25 km (15 miles) an hour. An average of ten hurricanes a year spawn in the Caribbean and South Atlantic—but few of these violent tropical storms ever reach land, so you're unlikely to experience a hurricane. Although the season runs from mid-June to mid-November, nearly all of them arrive in August or September.

Two great hurricanes have struck Miami. In September of 1926 a slow-moving storm raked the city with hurricane-force winds for 24 hours, killing hundreds of people and putting an end to the Florida boom. In August 1992 Hurricane Andrew struck with winds estimated at up to 320 km (200 miles) an hour, wreaking billions of dollars of damage. However, most of the affected areas were in the southern suburbs, so few tourist-oriented areas were damaged.

These days, sophisticated tracking systems give people plenty of time to batten down and take shelter. When the weatherman announces a "hurricane watch," it means a storm may be heading towards the coast. A "hurricane warning" is given 24 hours before the storm is expected to hit.

when a new lighthouse was built farther out to sea, and then exactly 100 years later reactivated to guide small craft into the Cape Florida channel.

Cloisters of the Monastery of St. Bernard de Clairvaux, 16711 West Dixie Highway, North Miami Beach. While shopping in Europe for art works in the 1920s, William Randolph Hearst picked up this 12th-century building at a bargain price of $50,000. He thought it would make a nice setting for his swimming pool at San Simeon. The cloisters were duly dismantled, the stones packed in straw and shipped to New York in 10,000 numbered crates.

With foot-and-mouth disease raging in Spain, the U.S. Department of Agriculture ordered the crates opened and the straw—a possible source of contamination—destroyed. During the operation many of the stones were returned to the wrong crates. Hearst consigned "the greatest jigsaw puzzle in history" to a warehouse for the next 25 years.

In 1952, two Miami entrepreneurs reassembled the Early Gothic structure. The Cuban tile floors are modern (somebody forgot to pack the original ones) and the armorial corbels are antique replacements. Otherwise the cloisters are authentic in every detail, down to the well in the patio and the wrought-iron gate at the entrance to the gardens. The Episcopal diocese of South Florida holds church services at the cloisters on Sunday and Wednesday mornings. At other times the property is open to visitors.

Coral Gables Merrick House and Gardens, 907 Coral Way; Tel. (305) 460-5361; grounds, daily; house, Sunday, 2:00 P.M.–5:00 P.M.; fee for house. This coral-rock dwelling was the only house for miles when the pioneering Merrick family moved in at the turn of the century. Many of the original furnishings are on view, together with memorabilia of the Coral Gables plantation, a grapefruit concern operated

by George Merrick's father, Solomon, a retired Congrega-
tional minister.

Life here was cosy for the Merricks, who imported their
Pianola and devotional books to the Florida frontier. Merrick
spent the evening hours perusing *Fox's Book of Martyrs,*
while his wife, Althea, worked at her needlepoint and dab-
bled in oils. Paintings by Althea and her youngest son,
Richard, decorate an upstairs bedroom, along with oils by
her brother, Denman Fink—hired by George Merrick as
artistic adviser to the city of Coral Gables. The municipal
charter was signed out in the garden, under the shade of a
spreading rubber tree.

The house is open to the public on Wednesdays and Sunday afternoons.

Coral Castle of Florida, 28655 South Dixie Highway,
Tel. (305) 248-6344; daily, 9:00 A.M.–6:00 P.M.; fee. Promot-
ers tout this South Dade landmark as a cross between Stone-
henge and the Great Pyramid. An immigrant from Latvia
named Edward Leedskalnin built the coral-rock house, as
well as its solid-rock furniture and monolithic sculptural
groups, singlehandedly between 1920 and 1940.

He was a frail man, no more than 153 cm (5 feet) tall, yet
somehow he managed to excavate, carve, and position huge
blocks of coral rock. Leedskalnin never allowed anyone to
see him at work, and to this day no one can quite figure out
how he did it.

THE EVERGLADES

It's not an accessible landscape. Just an awesome flatness,
relieved by dense tufts of hardwood hammock—islands of
green in the "River of Grass." Silence enfolds you. Plumed
clouds drift in an empty sky. Here in the Everglades you lux-
uriate in space and quiet.

Everglades National Park covers the southern tip of Florida, an area of more than 5,180 sq km (2,000 square miles); the Everglades region is vaster still, extending as far as Lake Okeechobee. A sheet of water 80 km (50 miles) wide flows southwards from the lake to Florida Bay and the Gulf of Mexico. It moves imperceptibly through that flat, flat terrain, which slopes just as imperceptibly downwards.

In summer and autumn—the rainy season—the water level in this great conduit rises, though much less now than formerly. Decades of drainage and "water management"

have dried out the glades, upsetting the fragile balance of nature. Concerned citizens propose restoring the free flow of water in order to "Save Our Everglades."

Like Mt. Everest, the Serengeti Plain, and Galapagos Islands, the Everglades is a World Heritage Site. The pinelands, hammocks, and sawgrass prairie shelter some of the rarest birds and animals on earth, including the great white heron and southern bald eagle, the Florida panther and crocodile, and the Everglades mink. More than 40 kinds of plants are unique to the area.

The best time to visit the park is winter or spring, when the concentration of animal and bird life is at its greatest—and

Glades Guidelines

- Mosquitoes and other biting insects can be annoying, above all in summer. Wear a hat, loose, long-sleeved shirt, and trousers. Use plenty of repellent—and no perfume. It attracts mosquitoes as honey does bees.
- Don't approach birds or animals or attempt to feed them. Alligators, in particular, appear deceptively lethargic.
- Avoid contact with toxic plants, such as poison ivy, poisonwood, and manchineel.
- Beware of poisonous snakes: water moccasins, coral snakes, diamond-back and pygmy rattlesnakes.
- Swimming is prohibited. Alligators and water moccasins lurk in freshwater ponds; crocodiles and barracuda cruise offshore waters.
- To hike off the trails, apply at one of the Visitor Centers for a back-country permit.
- Freshwater fishing is allowed in designated areas with a licence.
- Pets are banned from nature trails and amphitheatres.

when insects are at their least bothersome. Everglades National Park remains open 24 hours a day, all year round. There are two access routes from Miami: southwest via the Turnpike Extension and Route 9336 to the Main Entrance (56 km/35 miles), and west 40 km (25 miles) along Tamiami Trail (U.S. 41) to Shark Valley, open to pedestrians, cyclists, and tram passengers only.

You'll see a much larger section of the park if you take the southwesterly route, but a trip to Shark Valley can be combined with a visit to Coopertown and the Miccosukee Indian Village.

The Road to Flamingo

Before you go into the park, stop at the temporary **Visitor Center** to see the excellent 15-minute introductory film on the Everglades prepared by the National Park Service. Don't forget to pick up a free map and information about organised activities.

A road runs 61 km (38 miles) from the entrance to Flamingo on Florida Bay. All along the way, turn-offs lead to viewing areas where raised platforms, boardwalks, and signposted footpaths take you safely into the wilderness. If time is short (half a day or less), concentrate on the Gumbo Limbo, Anhinga, and Pa-hay-Okee Overlook trails, which offer the most in the way of landscape and wildlife close to the entrance.

Off the main road to the left, the **Gumbo Limbo Trail** makes a 1 km (half-mile) circuit through a hammock, or tropical forest, of mahogany, wild coffee, and native gumbo limbo trees. Plaques identify the vegetation. They call the

Flamingos flock together at the waterline, adding a dash of unexpected color to the verdant landscape.

gumbo limbo the "tourist tree" because its bark turns red and peels. The poisonwood tree looks as noxious as it is: hideous orange spots cover the trunk like a canker. Early in the morning and late at night, otters, raccoons, opossums—even bobcats and white-tailed deer—wander this way. But the witching hour comes late in the afternoon, when pinpoints of light shine diamond-bright through the dense canopy of leaves.

The nearby **Anhinga Trail** swings out across the saw grass and over a slough, or freshwater channel. This is the best place in the park to view animals and birds at close quarters. You'll come across alligators, marsh rabbits, egrets and, of course, anhingas. On the **Pineland Trail** you penetrate a dense stand of tall, slender-shafted Dade County pines, habitat of the rare Florida panther. Fifty years ago, much of Dade County looked like this.

Across Rock Reef Pass (altitude 1 metre/three feet), the **Pa-hay-Okee Overlook Trail** offers an intimate view of the sawgrass prairie that Marjory Stoneman Douglas describes in her Florida classic, *The Everglades: River of Grass.* Although "Pa-hay-Okee" means "River of Grass," the sawgrass is not a grass, but a sedge—an older and more primitive plant form. Grasses abound at Pa-hay-Okee, too: arrowhead, Muhly grass, Everglades beardgrass.

Past more halting places—Mahogany Hammock, Paurotis Pond, Hell's Bay (hell for canoers), Nine Mile Pond—

A is for Anhinga

The Anhinga Trail takes its name from a curious bird with a snake-like neck and tail feathers that resemble a turkey's. Alas, poor anhinga, its oil glands are not sufficient for its needs. The bird gets literally soaked to the skin when it dives into the water, and it has to hang itself up to dry.

you come to **Flamingo,** centre for fishing, hiking, and boating expeditions. Rooms at the inn, as well as self-catering cottages and campsites, are very much in demand in the winter season, so try to book ahead. The marina supplies everything from bait and tackle to fully equipped houseboats for hire.

A memorial outside the Visitor Center honours Guy Bradley, an Audubon warden who died here in the line of duty in 1905. He was killed by poachers hunting egrets for their feathers, a practice outlawed in 1903 as the species neared extinction.

Gliding on the glades—visitors enjoy an airboat ride across the Everglades.

Look through one of the telescopes on the breezeway and you'll see descendants of the birds he gave his life to save, preening themselves just offshore in their protected rookeries.

A sunset cruise of Florida Bay is the perfect way to end an Everglades day.

Exploring the Trail

About 25 km (15 miles) from Miami, **Coopertown** is home to the Kennon clan, operators of the original Everglades **airboat ride,** one of Florida's transcendent tourist experiences. From first light into the night, the Kennons will take you through canals teeming with alligators, where huge sheafs of saw grass sheer up out of the water and white birds flap darkly in the sky.

Airboats can travel in as little as half an inch of water, opening up areas of the glades that no conventional motor

Alligators and other swamp-dwellers populate the vast stretch of the Everglades.

craft could reach. When water levels allow, you'll cross the sawgrass prairie to hammocks that attract egrets, herons, ibis, and the elusive purple gallinule, an iridescent beauty that pads about on clumsy yellow feet—rather like an elegantly dressed woman in trainers.

Farther along the Trail, the walk-in gate at **Shark Valley** remains open round the clock. You can trek up to 25 km (15 miles) on the Loop Road to the Everglades Observation Tower or stroll in leisurely fashion to Bobcat Hammock, Otter Cave, or Heron View, where wading birds like the roseate spoonbill are wont to gather. Two-hour ranger-led tram tours depart every hour in season.

The Miccosukee tribe of Indians claims the Everglades as its homeland. Reduced at one time by war and removal to a band of 50 souls, the tribe now numbers 500. Like the better-known Seminoles, the Miccosukees are a branch of the Creek nation, but while the Seminoles speak the Muskogee language, the Miccosukees converse in Mikasuki. (The two tongues are mutually unintelligible.) The Miccosukees continued to follow a traditional lifestyle until the 1920s—longer than any other tribe in the United States. Even now they strive to preserve their identity and their traditions.

The big attraction at the **Miccosukee Indian Village** is the alligator arena, where muscular braves wrestle mean-looking reptiles in daily shows. Like bullfighters and motor-racing drivers, they're nonchalant about the dangers of their chosen sport. A tour of the village involves craft demonstrations, such as basket weaving and patchwork, and a look at the artefacts in the small museum. A couple of Indian families actually live on the premises, taking up residence in their cool, thatched "chickees" when the last of the tourists go home. A neighbouring amenity is the **Great Cypress National Preserve.** The biggest of the bald cypress trees here have seen 700 summers.

WHAT TO DO

Although the beach comes first for most people, Miami offers tourist activities of many other kinds.

SPORTS

Virtually all warm-weather sports are catered for. The resort hotels have swimming pools, tennis, and shuffleboard courts. A few maintain golf greens on the premises. A source of information for sports in Miami and throughout Florida is the Florida Sports Foundation, 107 W. Gaines Street, Talahassee, FL 23299, Tel. (904) 488-8347. The foundation publishes guides on golf, fishing, boating, and many other sports.

Watersports

Bay beaches are best for windsurfing and water-skiing, ocean beaches for swimming. For an up-to-the-minute weather report, including full details of wind, sea, and sun-tanning conditions, call the Weather Line: (305) 669-9111 (24-hour service).

Swimming. Although right of way to the beach may be private, the shore is public property to the high water line.

Ease of access makes Miami Beach popular with Miamians. Try the swinging 21st Street Beach or the expansive swimming area at 46th, set right in the middle of the great resort hotels. There's a place in the sun for the public at 53rd, 64th, and 72nd to 74th streets. North Shore Open Space Park Beach (79th to 87th streets) has the most elaborate facilities, with a fitness course, boardwalk, and thatched shelters in an attractive setting of palm trees and sea grape. Possibilities farther north include the beaches at Surfside, Bal Harbour, and Sunny Isles.

Key Biscayne's beaches are the clear favourite of local swimmers and sunbathers. Crandon Park has snack bars, picnic facilities, a bath house, and cabanas to let by the day, week or month, while Cape Florida provides plenty of picnic tables and grills under the pines.

Jellyfish, Portuguese man-of-war, and sting rays can present a hazard to swimmers on Atlantic beaches, but they won't bother you if you leave them alone. In the rare event of a man-of-war invasion (usually after a heavy storm), life guards advise swimmers to keep out of the water.

On a lucky day you can escape the crowds for fun in the sun on one of Miami's many beaches.

Outstanding among municipal swimming centres is historic Venetian Pool in Coral Gables (see pages 44).

Windsurfing. The most popular spot in town is off Rickenbacker Causeway, between the toll gate and Seaquarium, followed by Dinner Key. Some hotels and half a dozen specialised dealers rent equipment.

Water-skiing. If your hotel doesn't have boats or skiing gear, you can fit yourself out at one of the ski centres along the Rickenbacker and 79th Street causeways. For a real thrill, try jet-skiing around the bay.

Surfing. The biggest rollers come in to shore at South Pointe and Haulover Beach.

Boating. Oceanfront hotels generally have a flotilla of catamarans and sunfish sailing boats for hire, while several firms at Dinner Key in Coconut Grove and at the Miami Beach Marina rent sailing boats by the hour, half-day, day, and week. If you've never sailed before, the protected waters of Biscayne Bay make a good place to learn. Most hire companies advise beginners to complete at least six hours of instruction before going out alone.

Motor boats are available at Pelican Harbor Marina on the 79th Street Causeway, Crandon Marina on Key Biscayne, and Flamingo Marina in Everglades National Park.

Canoeing is popular in the Everglades, but some trails need more skill than others—notably Hell's Bay and the Wilderness Waterway. You can rent a canoe by the hour at the Flamingo Marina, although Everglades Canoe Outfitters, just outside the national park entrance, offers the most complete service.

Snorkelling. Mask and flippers open up an exotic underwater world of sponges, sea whips, soft corals, spiny lobsters, crabs, and rainbow-bright tropical fish. At the northern limit of Florida's coral reef, Biscayne National Park is the best place to snorkel in Dade County. Unless you're experienced, stay on the patch, or fringing reefs, close to shore: currents can be strong on the outer barrier reef. Hire a boat and skipper it yourself, or join an organised excursion aboard the *Reef Rover III*).

Snorkellers and divers must display a warning flag while they are below the surface. It is illegal to remove coral from the sea bed.

Scuba-diving. You can dive down to a wreck in Biscayne National Park, or explore the shallow reefs off Key Biscayne. Other likely places include the waters around Fowey Rock, Elbow, Pacific, and Carysfort lighthouses. Various shops rent equipment, arrange for tuition, and organise excursions.

Fishing. You can fish the bay waters from causeways and bridges where catwalks are provided, or cast your line into the Atlantic from beaches or piers such as the popular ones at Haulover Beach Park and Sunny Isles.

Deep-sea fishing excursions offer a fine diversion from the hustle and bustle of the city.

As for deep-sea fishing, you can charter a private boat or join a group of fishermen on a "party boat" for a reasonable fee per person (rods provided for a small extra charge). For the names of charter companies, private and group, look in the *Yellow Pages* under "Fishing Parties."

Other Sports

There are endless possibilities for active participation throughout the year in Miami.

Golf. The municipalities and Dade County Parks and Recreation Department maintain some popular public courses, including the scenic Key Biscayne Golf Links—voted Florida's best public course. Certain clubs, like the famous Doral, open their greens to non-members. Although not every hotel has a course of its own, many can arrange for their guests to play at a private club. For further information on golfing, consult the brochure "Golf is Greater in Miami," available from the Greater Miami Convention & Visitors Bureau, or the "Official Florida Golf Guide," from the Florida Sports Foundation.

Tennis. With more than 400 courts in the metropolitan area, Miami is indeed tennis country. Apart from all the hotel courts, you can play at any of a number of public tennis centres, including Flamingo Park in the Art Deco District and North Shore Open Space Park.

Cycling. More than 209 km (130 miles) of paved bike paths make the going good in Miami. You can sightsee by bike on Key Biscayne, where shady paths cross the island. Ride out to Fairchild Tropical Garden or the Parrot Jungle from Coconut Grove, taking the banyan-lined path that parallels Old Cutler Road. Or combine birdwatching and bike riding at Shark Valley in the Glades (see page 77).

Jogging. You can do it in a park—David Kennedy Park in the Grove is a local favourite—or barefoot on the beach.

Or, if you don't want to get your toes wet, go jogging along Miami Beach's oceanfront boardwalk.

Hiking. Everglades National Park is the place to go. Join a group or strike out on your own. Ask at the Visitor Centre about nature trails and back-country destinations.

Hunting. Turkey shoots are a Coopertown speciality. And so is frogging, which is strictly a nighttime occupation. The Kennons will provide you with a gig, head lamp, and their considerable expertise (see page 76).

Spectator Sports

In sports-mad Miami, there is no shortage of competitive events.

Motor Racing. The Miami Grand Prix in February attracts the best drivers on the international circuit. The race is run on the six-lane sweep of Biscayne Boulevard and in Bicentennial Park downtown.

Horse Racing. Hialeah Park (see pages 60) and Gulfstream, in Broward County, share winter dates in rotation. North Miami's Calder track opens for the summer season. Established in the 1920s, Hialeah has a thoroughly patrician air. Calder, by contrast, is newer and more functional, but it can produce champions like the Kentucky Derby winner, Spend-a-Buck, which started out here.

Dog Racing. Dog races are held every evening, in addition to several matinées a week. Biscayne Kennel Club in Miami Shores and Flagler Dog Track in the city of Miami open in turn.

Jai-alai (pronounced "high lie"). At the Miami Jai-Alai Fronton near the airport, in N.W. 37th Avenue, you can put bets on—or just watch—this exciting, fast-paced ball game from Spain's Basque country. Helmeted players use long-handled, scooped, basket-like *cestas* to hurl and catch the ball as it ricochets at fantastic speed around the three-walled court. Games take place every night except Sunday, and on certain afternoons in the winter and summer seasons.

Golf. If golf is your game, don't miss the Doral-Ryder Open Tournament, held at the Doral Golf Resort and Spa, or the Elizabeth Arden Classic at Turnberry Isle in January or February.

The Florida Marlins—champions of the 1997 World Series—can be seen at Pro Player Stadium.

Football. The Miami Dolphins—who are professional champions—play to capacity crowds in the Dolphin Stadium in North Dade County. Fans also turn out for the Orange Bowl for that winning varsity team, the University of Miami Hurricanes. Go for the experience, if not the game itself.

Baseball. The Florida Marlins, new to professional baseball in the 1992 season, won the World Series in 1997; they play in Pro Player Stadium, 27 km (16 miles) north of downtown. Spring training brings the Baltimore Orioles to Miami Stadium (2301 N.W. 10th Avenue) in March and April. See them play teams based elsewhere in Florida in the "Grapefruit League" games, a prelude to the summer season.

Speedboat Racing. Power-boating has long been a popular sport in Miami. Enquire locally for information about events.

SHOPPING

Miami is the sophisticated crossroads of the Caribbean, the place where all Latin America comes to shop.

If you're in the market for competitively priced electronic goods, gold jewellery, and clothing, then follow the crowds downtown to Flagler Street—or go bargain-hunting in the Miami Free Zone (N.W. 107th Street).

For ethnic items, explore the emporia of Calle Ocho in Little Havana, as well as the small shops in Coconut Grove, where merchants stock all kinds of pottery, handicrafts, and imports.

Some of the best window shopping in town is along Decorator's Row (40th Street between N.E. 2nd Avenue and Miami Avenue). Showrooms here display furniture, fixtures, and fittings garnered from across the nation and around the world. Certain establishments open their doors "to the trade only," but an air of confidence will generally carry you across the threshold.

For the most part, Miami's department and chain stores are concentrated in vast, air-conditioned malls like North Miami's Aventura and Dadeland (largest in the Southeast), off U.S. 1 in North Kendall Drive. The exclusive big stores (Neiman Marcus, Bonwit Teller, Saks Fifth Avenue, Lord and Taylor, Bloomingdale's) and designer boutiques have premises in the prestige malls of Bal Harbour and The Falls in South Dade—all distinguished by their inventive architecture, landscaping, and display.

Check in the local papers for details of sales and special offers. Or shop in Fashion District outlets (N.W. 5th Avenue between 24th and 29th streets) for all-year-round bargains in designer clothing and accessories and also for Miami-manufactured articles.

Best Buys

Prices can vary considerably, so shop around before you put your money down.

Active sportswear. American manufacturers lead the field when it comes to aerobic clothing and track suits, and the fanciful golf and tennis gear is guaranteed to enhance your image, even if it won't improve your game.

Children's clothing. Miami is an ideal place to buy American-style clothing for your children, including denims, overalls, and miniature track suits.

Cigars. Hand-rolled "Havanas" made in Miami are practically the authentic Cuban article.

Citrus fruit. Send yourself a crate of Florida oranges or grapefruit. Miami fruit shippers (including several concerns at the airport) air-freight fruit all over the U.S. and around the world.

Cosmetics and toiletries. Sun preparations include a sophisticated range of tanning lotions and some esoteric blocking ointments and creams for complete protection from ultra-violet rays. Locally made beauty products incorporate rejuvenating papaya enzymes and the healing sap of the aloe plant.

Electronics. You can choose from an array of Japanese and American-made cameras, computers, radios, and other goods. The prices are as interesting as the competition is keen.

Foodstuffs. Carry home the taste of the tropics in the form of Florida coconut patties, chocolate-covered citrus peel, and orange-blossom honey. If you appreciate the fine flavour and

Trendy shops and boutiques make Coconut Grove a shoppers' paradise.

rich aroma of Cuban-style coffee, it's worth stocking up with enough to last until your next trip—vacuum-packed in tins and lightweight plastic packets.

Gadgets. You'll find a variety of handy implements, from serrated grapefruit knives to a special plastic straw that enables you to drink juice direct from an orange.

Indian handicraft. Miccosukee craftswomen fashion traditional patchwork garments, beaded necklaces, and palmetto-fibre dolls—all available at the Indian village on the Tamiami Trail (see pages 77).

Jewellery. Look for adornments of shell, glass, and semi-precious stones—or the narrow gold bangle bracelets that Cuban women favour.

Beautifully woven tapestries are available for purchase at the Miccosukee Indian Village.

Linens. Designer collections for the bed and bath combine ease of care with original styling.

Resort clothing. American designers pioneered the casual look, and they still do it better than anyone else. Be as traditional or as trendy as you like in tropical whites, pastel linens, and bright cottons. Some of the most famous American designers produce inexpensive lines with designer flair, including Calvin Klein and others.

Shoes. Imports from Brazil, Argentina, and elsewhere in South America are reasonably priced.

Souvenirs. These run the gamut from magnetic seashells and driftwood lampstands to plastic alligators; take your pick.

Swimwear. Miami lives at the beach. The range of sizes and styles is almost infinite.

Western gear. From hats, boots, and bandanas to silver-studded belts, Miami outfitters supply both Dade County dudes and urban cowboys.

ENTERTAINMENT

A good way to keep up with Miami's lively entertainment scene is to check out the Friday weekend section of the *Miami Herald* newspaper or *Miami Today* or *New Times*, or both weeklies that are distributed for free.

After dark, three venues are especially popular, both with Miamians and their visitors. South Beach, with its sidewalk cafés, restaurants, and night clubs, is the premier night district of Miami. Ocean Drive at night becomes a sea of strollers vying for seats at outdoor tables and admiring the scenery, both human and natural. Coconut Grove, especially the CocoWalk complex, attracts a young crowd to its compact, gas-lit downtown of cafés, bars, and boutiques. And the Bayside complex, on the bayfront in downtown Miami, has food courts, shops, and nightly entertainment.

Flamenco shows are popular in Little Havana, and in season a couple of major hotels on the Beach still put on lavish floor shows with chorus lines, name entertainers, and comedy acts.

There are lots of discos, some with live groups. Piano bars specialize in mood music, drinks, and, perhaps, dinner. Lively cocktail lounges have jazz combos, rock groups, or soul or pop singers on hand. Romantic trios play in the lounges of the more elegant hotels, where sedate couples may be seen dancing cheek to cheek.

Latin music is featured at the many outdoor festivals held in and around Miami

Broadway hits come to Coconut Grove Playhouse, while the big Broadway musicals open at the Jackie Gleason Theater of the Performing Arts. As for open-air performances, the South Florida Theater Company brings Shakespeare to the elegant gardens of Vizcaya for two months every winter.

Teatro Avante and other Hispanic theatre groups stage both popular and experimental plays. You'll have a fascinating evening ahead of you, if your Spanish is up to it.

Concerts, both classical and popular, take place at the Dade County Auditorium, the Gusman Cultural Center, and the Jackie Gleason Theater of the Performing Arts on the Beach, as well as at local churches and temples.

From October to May, internationally renowned performers and orchestras come to town for the Prestige, Great Artists, and International Artists series. Throughout the year, the Performing Arts for Community and Education authority (P.A.C.E.) organises excellent free events such as the popular Big Orange Festival. There's also a season of opera, presented in English (national series) and the original language (international series) by the Greater Miami Opera.

The leading American modern dance companies make regular appearances here. You'll also have the chance to see the Miami City Ballet and other local groups, such as the Momentum Dance Company, which features new work by Florida choreographers. In another vein, the Ballet Concerto Company perpetuates the traditions of the Cuban National Ballet.

Cinemas all over town screen the popular Hollywood blockbusters. Art houses such as the Arcadia, Beaumont, and Cinematheque in the Gables, as well as the Grove Cinema, show classic and avant-garde films from around the world; Little Havana specialises in Spanish-language diversions. Consult the schedules in the daily newspapers.

Calendar of Events

January	*Three Kings' Parade.* Little Havana steps out on the Sunday nearest Epiphany (January 6).
	Art Deco Weekend. Vintage car rallies, jazz concerts, exhibitions and tours, and fancy-dress balls on Miami Beach recreate the mood of the Gatsby era.
	Coconut Grove Arts Festival. A major fête with arts and crafts, fine art, entertainment, and foods.
	Miami Grand Prix. On the downtown Miami streets.
February /March	*Carnaval Miami.* Ten days of Latin-style festivities, climaxing in Calle Ocho Open House, a street party in Little Havana attended by almost a million people.
	Italian Renaissance Festival. Chain-mail garment makers, bookbinders, and madrigal singers do their thing at Vizcaya. Italian food, music, and dancing.
	Salute to Canada Week. The resort of Surfside fêtes holidaymakers from north of the border with a programme of theatre, concerts, and sporting events.
June	*Bahamas Goombay Festival.* Descendants of Coconut Grove's original settlers recall the food, music, and crafts of their island of origin.
July	*All American Celebration.* Miami Beach throws a big party on the Fourth of July. Free concerts are a highlight of the oceanside revels.
October	*Baynanza.* Attention turns to Biscayne Bay for a week of events that include the Columbus Day regatta and fairs at Haulover Park and the Port of Miami.
November	*Florida Renaissance Fayre.* See knights jousting on Key Biscayne or watch a play of the period.
December	*Miccosukee Indian Arts Festival.* Music, dance, and art when Indian tribes from throughout the Americas get together at the Miccosukee village.
December /January	*Orange Bowl Festival.* Not one event but many. Culminates in the King Orange Jamboree Parade nighttime extravaganza.

EATING OUT

The possibilities for experimentation have burgeoned with the expanding population. You can sample Southern home cooking as authentic as any this side of the Mason-Dixon line and kosher fare to compare with New York's best. But the real gastronomic news in Miami is the explosion of interest in ethnic food—Cuban cuisine first and foremost, but also Mexican, Haitian, Nicaraguan, Argentine, Greek, Indian, Japanese, and Thai.

South Dade farmers supply chefs with a bounty of fresh fruit and vegetables, and offshore waters provide plenty of fish and shellfish. Everglades frog legs turn up on some menus, and you may just come across alligator meat. It's farmed out in the glades, though consumption is, for the time being, limited.

Meal Times

Most restaurants serve breakfast from 7:00 to 11:00 A.M., and lunch from about 11:30 to 1:30 P.M. or so. Dinner is available from 5:00 or 6:00 P.M. until 10:00 or 11:00 P.M., with the exception of Little Havana establishments and a few others on the Beach, which don't close down till midnight or 1:00 in the morning—and even later at weekends.

Some restaurants offer an "early bird special"—a menu at a pre-theatre reduced price—to diners who order their evening meal before 6:00 P.M. A brunch menu is widely available on Sundays from 11:00 A.M. to 3:00 P.M. If hunger strikes in the middle of the night, make for one of the chain coffee shops, open 24 hours.

Where To Eat

Miami's best restaurants are concentrated in the Gables, the Grove, and the Beach (especially in South Beach these days). You can dine on the oceanfront, in sight of the sea, in Art-Deco surroundings or a garden setting, or around an open hearth. Gamble while you eat at the race track, dog track, or jai-alai fronton. Or have a meal at one of the theme restaurants that evoke medieval Spain or Tudor England.

In the more elegant establishments, jacket or jacket and tie are required, but for the most part you can cultivate a casual appearance. A lot of oceanfront hotels ban improperly attired swimmers from indoor restaurants, so be prepared with shoes and appropriate clothing.

Coffee shops serve sandwiches, salads, light meals, and snacks—but no alcohol. If you're in a hurry, sit at the counter for faster service.

Delicatessens specialise in sandwiches, pastries, and kosher dishes. Long queues form outside the popular delis at peak hours, but they generally move quickly. If you don't want to wait, put in your order "to go." There's usually a special window or queue for take-out service.

Fast-food outlets include local ethnic franchises, usually to be found at the big shopping centres. Order from the counter of your choice—Greek, Italian, Cuban, Japanese, whatever—and take a seat afterwards in the central courtyard.

Juice bars feature fruit and vegetable juices, including fresh-squeezed orange and grapefruit. Have a *piña colada*— pineapple juice and coconut milk—without the rum.

Healthfood restaurants emphasize fruit and vegetable preparations, though some do serve fish. The produce used is often organically grown.

Cafeterias cater to people on a budget or in a hurry. You take a tray and choose your meal from a selection of hot and cold dishes. Items that are cooked to order will be brought to you when they're ready. At some cafeterias you carry your tray to the table yourself. At others, a waiter performs this service, for which he expects a small tip. Usually you pay the cashier as you leave.

Eating Habits

For Europeans, certain American customs may be unfamiliar, if not downright bewildering. The predilection for ice in drinks, for example, causes consternation. Nothing escapes the cold treatment, from whisky to cola. If you prefer your drinks cool, but not iced, remember to say so when you order.

The coffee ritual (like the coffee itself) takes a bit of getting used to. Unless it's Cuban-style, the brew is weak by European standards—and the cup is "bottomless." That means the waiter will refill it repeatedly without extra charge.

Don't be surprised if your waiter urges you to take your leftovers home in a "doggie bag." Some restaurants serve far

The bay offers a pleasant backdrop for outdoor dining in Coconut Grove.

more than one person can eat—on the assumption that customers will carry away what they don't consume on the spot. Even cafeterias supply doggie bags, but you have to wrap up the food yourself.

What To Eat

In Miami, you can indulge in gastronomic experimentation all through the day.

Breakfast. Start the day right at a deli with coffee and a Danish, a kind of sweet roll with a prune, cinnamon-and-nut, or cream cheese filling. If you can't make up your mind, order an assortment of mini-Danishes and try them all. Or opt for bagels (whole-wheat bagels for the health-conscious!) with butter or cream cheese and jam.

Cuban street counters provide a compelling alternative in the form of guava pastries hot from the oven *(pastelitos de guayaba)* or toasted Cuban bread. If you like your coffee strong, a Cuban breakfast is the only breakfast. Have an eye-opening *café cubano*, strong and black, or *café con leche*, coffee with milk and sugar. Specify "no sugar" if you prefer coffee unsweetened.

The American option—"eggs any style"—comes Southern-style with grits (a cornmeal gruel) or with traditional home fries (sliced, sautéed potatoes) or hash brown potatoes (grated and fried with onion).

Brunch. This hybrid of breakfast and lunch leans more towards the former, though alcohol is admissible, especially a morning pick-me-up such as a Screwdriver or Bloody Mary. You can eat any breakfast food, though the classic dish is eggs Benedict—poached eggs and ham on English muffins (rather like a crumpet), topped with Hollandaise sauce. Seafood pancakes and chicken à la reine (in a cream sauce with mushrooms) are popular for brunch, too. A lot of Miami hotels feature a brunch buffet on Sundays.

Sandwiches. The deli variety includes corned beef, turkey, roast beef, smoked tongue, and pastrami (a kind of cured beef) stacked on your choice of bread—white, whole wheat, rye, pumpernickel, or rolls. Lox (smoked salmon) and cream cheese are a popular Jewish combination, served on a bagel.

Pita or Arab flat bread may be filled with tuna (tunny), egg, or chicken salads. A club sandwich is a layered collation of chicken, bacon, tomato, and lettuce, with mayonnaise, on toast.

You'll have a job stretching your mouth around a Cuban sandwich—it's piled so high with sugar-cured ham, pork, Swiss cheese (an American original), and pickles. Leave it to the Cubans to improve on the hamburger: the *frita* adds minced pork to the beef, as well as garlic, paprika, vinegar, and spices.

Soups. Black-bean soup is a Cuban favorite, usually served with rice, and Spanish gazpacho is on many menus.

Chicken soup is more than a food; it's the home remedy every Jewish mother prescribes for all ills. Add a matzoh-meal dumpling to the broth and you have nourishing matzoh-ball soup.

Salads. The standard sort consists of shredded mixed greens or iceberg lettuce and sliced tomatoes with a choice of dressing: creamy, tomato-flavoured French, Russian (mayonnaise, tomato ketchup), Thousand Island (mayonnaise, chili sauce, pickle relish), Italian (oil, vinegar, garlic, herbs), and Roquefort.

Cole slaw is often served with hamburgers, sandwiches, or fried fish. Usually the shredded cabbage and carrot are mixed with mayonnaise, but a sweet vinaigrette dressing may also be used. Many restaurants feature a self-service salad bar, laden with greens and a variety of garnishes.

A salad can be a meal in itself. A Chef's Salad combines ham, turkey, tongue, roast beef or other cold meats, and sliced tomatoes on a bed of iceberg lettuce. Raw spinach salad is topped with sliced onion, mushrooms, and hard-boiled egg. Popular with garlic lovers, Caesar Salad blends crisp romaine lettuce and hard-boiled egg with croutons in a garlic-flavoured parmesan dressing.

Florida fruit salads are frequently—but not always—composed of fresh fruit. Depending on the season, you may be served a medley of mango, papaya, starfruit, grapefruit, orange, watermelon, and cantaloupe with your choice of frozen yogurt, sherbet (sorbet), or cottage cheese. Southerners are fond of ambrosia—sugared orange slices and grated fresh coconut.

Meat. Miami's steak houses and American-style establishments cater to the national passion for thick sirloin steaks and prime ribs.

Cuban flavour spills brightly onto the sidewalks of Little Havana.

Open-hearth restaurants specialise in tangy barbecued ribs—usually baby beef—grilled over hot coals.

Old-world chicken in the pot (boiled chicken) and beef flanken (boiled beef) are great kosher favourites. Chicken and dumplings (chicken stew and dumplings) and baked Virginia ham come straight from the old plantation.

Fish and shellfish. Order the catch of the day—flaky white Florida snapper, grouper, or sea trout grilled, fried, or sautéed in butter. The more delicate pompano is often prepared *en papillote* (baked in paper), a procedure that enhances the subtle flavour. You can eat the delicious dolphinfish (mahi mahi) with impunity; it bears no relation to Flipper and his friends. New England scrod often appears on local menus. It's usually fresh, but it's not from Florida. Hush puppies (fried balls of cornmeal and onion) may accompany fried fish and shellfish.

At a deli, have gefilte fish, a mixture of whitefish, egg, and matzoh meal, eaten cold or, occasionally, hot. Some restaurants will cook your own catch of the day for you if you clean the fish first. The service charge usually includes all the trimmings.

Fresh jumbo shrimps (and not all shrimps are fresh, even in Florida) usually come from the Gulf. Cold shrimp dishes include shrimp cocktail with red sauce (chilli sauce and horseradish), shrimp salad with mayonnaise dressing, and shrimp Louis with hard-boiled egg and Russian dressing. Shrimps are good skewered and grilled, breaded and sautéed with garlic (in which case they're called scampi), or deep-fried with tartare sauce. If you're not counting calories, indulge in seafood Newburg, a combination of shrimps, scallops, and lobster in a rich, tomato-flavoured cream sauce.

Lobster in Miami usually means the crawfish or Florida lobster. The taste and texture of this warm-water crustacean are distinctive—and no less delectable to the initiated. Ask for it boiled with lemon and butter sauce, and savour the nut-like flavour to the full.

Oysters and clams are served raw on the half shell, baked, or fried. But the big treat is Florida stone crabs, in season from October 15 to April 15. You eat only the claws—one is taken from the crab, which is returned to the water to grow another —hot with lemon and butter or cold with mustard mayonnaise. Most restaurants crack the shell well with a wooden mallet before serving, so you probably won't need the battery of implements you'll be given to extract the sweet meat. But it can be a messy business, so don't be surprised if your waiter produces a big paper bib and ties it round you toddler fashion.

Some restaurants that serve seafood propose a cold seafood platter featuring a selection of stone crab, shrimps, clams, oysters, and Florida lobster—or a fried Fisherman's Platter, including shrimps, oysters, scallops, clams, and fish fingers.

Vegetables. Satisfy a craving for the fresh variety at healthfood restaurants, where mixed vegetables are lightly steamed or stir-fried. Southern cooks have a way of their own with vegetables. Try stewed tomatoes (cooked with bread and a pinch of sugar), fried eggplant (aubergine), creamed onions, and candied yams (sweet potatoes glazed with sugar).

Desserts. Creamy, calorific Key lime pie is a South Florida original. The real thing contains the fresh juice of Key limes and, like the fruit, is yellow, not green. A meringue topping is traditional. Southern pecan pie plays havoc with the waist-line, too. The pecans are folded into a sweet mixture of corn syrup and egg yolk that's cloying to some, divine to others. Cheesecake reigns supreme among deli delights. And American apple pie is no stranger to Miami. Go all the way and have it "à la mode," with a scoop of rich vanilla ice cream.

Cuban food. Little Havana is *the* place to experiment. While you're mulling over the menu, order a drink—some sangría, perhaps—with *tostones* (fried slices of green plantain chips), *boniatos mariquitas* (fried sweet potato), and *malanguitas* (similar to potato chips)—all usually made to order.

For starters, try *sopón marinero* (shellfish soup with rice, peas, and red pepper) or the more traditional black-bean soup *(sopa de frijoles negros)*, flavoured with olive oil, garlic, salt pork, and vinegar. Alternatives include *empanadas* —baked or fried meat pies filled with ham, chicken, pork, or sausage—and chicken, beef, or fish croquettes.

Cuban rice dishes are famous: *arroz con pollo* (chicken and saffron rice) and *arroz con camarones* (shrimps and saffron rice). *Piccadillo*—highly seasoned minced meat with red or green peppers, onion, tomatoes, and garlic—is a simple dish that can be very good if it's freshly made.

Chopped onion and wedges of lime always accompany grilled meats: *bistec de cerdo* (pork) or *hígado* (liver) and thinly sliced *palomilla*, the king of Cuban steaks. For real sustenance, choose *boliche mechado*, a kind of stew, or *carne asada*, roast meat in a sauce with potatoes.

The most popular accompaniments are fried ripe plantains *(plátanos fritos)* and white rice, or rice and black beans cooked together, a staple known as *moros* or *arroz moros*. *Yuca* and *malanga* are to Cubans what potatoes are to Anglos. The taste is fairly bland—until you add a generous dollop of *mojito criollo*, a piquant sauce made of sour orange juice, olive oil, and garlic.

Like your fellow diners, you may well find it difficult to resist dessert—be it *flan* (caramel custard), *tocino del cielo*, a very rich, very sweet confection made of sugar and egg yolks, or *buñuelos*, deep-fried pastries covered in syrup.

The Cubans of Miami are also partial to a Nicaraguan sweet known as *tres leches*, sponge cake saturated in the "three milks" of the title—whole, evaporated, and condensed.

Afterwards, a cup of strong Cuban-style coffee will set you up for the rest of the day or night, as the case may be.

Creole cooking. Restaurants in Little Haiti offer all the typical dishes, beginning with *griot*. Haitians can't get enough of this snack food, made of pork that's first boiled, then fried in its own fat. Spicy Creole stews may incorporate goat or conch, the latter known to the Haitians as *lambi*. To go with it, there's boiled corn meal, rice and beans, and fried plantains.

A speciality of neighbourhood juice bars, Haitian fruit sodas (syrup and seltzer water) include some exotic varieties, and there's no end to the different kinds of fresh, tropical fruit juices.

Drinks

People in Miami often order iced tea with their meals, and wine is growing in popularity. You can order domestic wine by the bottle, carafe, or glass. Cuban restaurants feature Spanish wines, sangría, and cider.

You'll find American beer blander and more highly carbonated than the European variety—and it's served ice-cold. Imported beers are widely available.

Some people drink cocktails with their food in lieu of wine. Others prefer to indulge during the late-afternoon "happy hour," when bars serve free snacks with drinks, or two drinks for the price of one.

Southern tipplers favour Kentucky bourbon, a mellow whisky that is distilled from corn, malt, and rye. You drink it neat, on the rocks, or with soda.

From the old Havana to the new Miami comes the *Cuba libre*, a combination of rum, lime juice, and cola. Another rum drink, the daiquiri, contains lemon juice and sugar.

Beware of the all-American dry martini—this blend of gin and dry vermouth packs a considerable punch.

INDEX

HANDY TRAVEL TIPS

An A–Z Summary of Practical Information

A

ACCOMMODATION (*See also* CAMPING)

Book a room downtown, on the beach, or in one of Miami's palmy suburbs. Whatever your budget, there's a wide variety of accommodation to choose from. Reservations for hotels and motels in Greater Miami can be made from 8 a.m. to 8 p.m. daily by dialling the Greater Miami Reservation System; tel. 1-800-356-8392 (U.S.) or 1-800-248-3380 (Canada).

Bear in mind that rooms are at a premium during the peak tourist season (December 15 to Easter), above all at Christmastime and during the Easter holiday period. Summer can be busy, too, and rooms may be hard to come by during the Fourth of July and Labor Day weekends. On the oceanfront, rooms with a sea view are always more expensive. Private bath, colour television, and air conditioning are standard. Most of the larger hotels employ a hall porter, referred to in the United States as a "bell captain."

Many hotel and motel chains make no charge for children under 18 sharing a room with their parents. Inquire about "family plans" when you book. Some establishments offer special rates to guests who take their meals on the premises: A.P. (American Plan) includes three meals a day, and M.A.P. (Modified American Plan) breakfast and lunch or dinner.

Certain luxury hotels have suites only—bedroom and sitting room with kitchenette. In some areas you'll see signs advertising "efficiencies" or "pullmanettes"—modest bed-sitting rooms with cooking facilities. A minimum stay may be required.

A tax of 11.5-12.5% is added to hotel and motel bills in Miami area cities, among them Miami, Miami Beach, Bal Harbour, and Surfside.

Most hotels request that guests leave their rooms by noon on the day of departure. Check-in time is usually 3 p.m.

Airport hotels. The Miami International Airport Hotel has its premises in the main terminal building, on Concourse E. A score of hotels situated on the perimeter of the airfield provide free mini-bus transport to and from the terminal.

Art-Deco hotels. A group of renovated oceanfront hotels from the Jazz Age attract a trendy young crowd to the Art Deco National Historic District on the south shore of Miami Beach.

Smaller and more personal than the newer beach resorts, these hotels feature 1930s-era atmosphere in sight of the sea. To make a reservation, contact Art Deco Hotels, 1224 Ocean Drive, Miami Beach, FL 33139-2030; tel. (305) 534-2136.

Youth accommodation. The Greater Miami area has one youth hostel, the Clay Hotel and International Hostel, 1438 Washington Avenue, Miami Beach, FL 33139; tel. (305) 534-2988.

AIRPORT

Conveniently situated just west of the city centre, Miami International Airport is about 15 minutes by car from the downtown district, and 25 minutes from Miami Beach. Served by more than 60 airlines, Miami International is one of the world's busiest airports.

The main terminal comprises two levels, divided into various concourses or zones, with domestic arrivals below and departures above. Currency exchange, a 24-hour information desk (Concourse E), telephones, luggage lockers, duty-free shops, and numerous other stores are to be found on the upper level, along with various bars, fast-food restaurants, snack bars, and newsstands. Baggage-claim areas (show your ticket stubs to the security guard on the way out) and car-hire agencies occupy the lower level.

An elevated "people mover" links the main terminal building to a satellite terminal for international flights. There are telephones, a restaurant, duty-free shops, and a newsstand. Processing is fast and courteous in the adjoining Customs and Immigration facility, where red and green channels are in operation.

Check-in procedure. Depending on your destination and airline, you may be able to check in for your flight and register your luggage at curbside. Arrive one hour before domestic flights, two hours before international departures.

Ground transport. There are always plenty of taxis on hand for the trip into town. The bright blue vehicles of the Airport Region Taxi Service (ARTS) carry passengers to nearby destinations for a low flat fare. Super Shuttle mini buses transport passengers to hotels at about a third of the price of a taxi. Municipal buses leave every 30 to 60 minutes from a stop outside the main terminal building; ask at the information desk for route maps and details of connections.

B

BICYCLE HIRE

If you avoid busy streets and keep a sharp eye out for Florida's very aggressive drivers, Miami may well be the best place in the world to cycle, but wearing a helmet is advised. There are 138 miles of paved paths to explore, including highly scenic routes in Coral Gables, Key Biscayne, and Coconut Grove. To hire a bike in the area of your choice, look in the *Yellow Pages* under "Bicycles-Renting." In addition to standard, three-, and ten-speed models, tandem bikes are often available. Bicycles may be hired by the hour, day, week, or month. You may have to pay a deposit or leave your driving licence or passport as a surety.

Out in Everglades National Park (Tamiami entrance), you can cycle along the 15-mile Shark Valley loop road, sighting rare birds and wildlife as you go. Standard bikes may be hired by the hour at the entrance gate.

C

CAMPING

Camp sites are few and far between in urban Miami. Florida Kampgrounds (KOA) maintains one commercial site in the greater metropolitan area (on the southern outskirts of the city, it has a heated pool and hot tub). Miami South KOA is between Route 997 and US 1. Miami South KOA, 20675 S.W. 162nd Avenue, Miami, FL 33187; tel. (305) 233-5300.

The Dade County Parks and Recreation Department administers the Larry and Penny Thompson Campground, a 240-acre pinewood preserve near Metrozoo. Tent sites and hook-ups for 240 caravans or recreational vehicles are available on a first come, first-served basis.

Larry and Penny Thompson Campground, 12451 S.W. 184th Street, Miami, FL 33177; tel. (305) 232-1049.

M.E. Thompson Park, 170th Street and NW 157th Avenue, Miami, FL; tel. (305) 821-5122.

Camp Owaissa Bauer, 17001 SW 264th Street, Homestead, FL; tel. (305) 247-6016.

Designed for the handicapped, Bird Drive Park and Therapeutic Campground features a Vita course for wheelchair-bound athletes and a swimming pool with a hydraulic lift, as well as a nature trail with hand rails for the blind. For details, contact Bird Drive Park and Therapeutic Campground, 9401 S.W. 72nd Avenue, Miami, FL; tel. (305) 665-5319.

There are various camping possibilities in the wilds of Dade County—but don't expect to commute to town. Farmland surrounds Southern Comfort Campground, near the Florida City entrance to Everglades National Park. In the park itself, camping is permitted at Long Pine Key and Flamingo. Areas for camping have also been set aside in Biscayne National Park and Chekika State Recreation Area. It's a good idea to reserve in advance. Maximum stay is two weeks. Mosquitoes are a nuisance in summer. Take repellent.

Southern Comfort RV Resort, 345 E. Palm Drive, Florida City, FL 33034; tel. (305) 248-6909.

Everglades National Park, 40001 State Road 9336, Homestead, FL 33034; tel. (305) 242-7700.

Biscayne National Park, P.O. Box 1369, Homestead, FL 33090-1369; tel. (305) 230-PARK.

Chekika State Recreation Area, S.W. 237th Avenue and Grossman Drive, Homestead, FL 33030; tel. (305) 251-0371.

Camping at the roadside, in a car park, or on private land without permission is both illegal and unsafe.

CAR HIRE

Rates in Miami are among the lowest in the United States, even during high season, so it pays to shop around before you hire a car. As you compare the prices of the national firms with those of the numerous local companies, check whether or not insurance cover is included. Rates fluctuate seasonally. Air conditioning is a standard feature.

To hire a car, you must be at least 21 years old and in possession of a valid driving licence. Some agencies make exceptions for 18-year-old drivers paying with their own credit cards. For tourists from non-English-speaking countries, a translation of the driving licence is highly recommended, together with the national licence itself, or, failing this, an International Driving Permit.

It will be more convenient to settle your bill with a credit card, rather than cash. If you have no card, you must leave a sizable cash deposit–and cash may not be accepted at night or on weekends.

CHILDREN

The family-oriented resort hotels organize supervised activities for children of all ages.

CIGARETTES, CIGARS, TOBACCO

Cigarettes may vary in price by as much as one third, depending where you obtain them. A packet from a vending machine always costs more than one bought in a supermarket or at a newsstand. The choice of pipe tobacco, both home-grown and imported, is vast. Cuban artisans still roll cigars by hand in Little Havana and cigar shops—some quite elegant—are popular elsewhere in Miami.

Signs prohibiting smoking are visible in a many public places. In restaurants, there are often smoking and no-smoking sections.

CLIMATE

Winter is the tourist season in sub-tropical South Florida. Days are warm and sunny and nights, pleasantly cool. Some years, the occasional cold spell can send temperatures plummeting to near freezing point for a day or two, but that's the exception, not the rule.

Most of the rainfall for the year occurs in summer, in late afternoon showers that cool the air. Summers in Miami may be hot and humid, but thanks to the trade winds they're rarely unbearable.

Average daytime temperatures:

		J	F	M	A	M	J	J	A	S	O	N	D
Maximum	°F	74	75	78	80	84	86	88	88	87	83	78	76
	°C	23	24	26	27	29	30	31	31	31	28	26	24
Minimum	°F	61	61	64	67	71	74	76	76	75	72	66	62
	°C	16	16	18	19	22	23	24	24	24	22	19	17

* Minimum temperatures are measured just before sunrise, maximum temperatures in the afternoon.

CLOTHING

Although daytime temperatures generally hover in the upper 70s Fahrenheit, they can soar higher—or dip lower. So be prepared for every eventuality with an assortment of lightweight and heavier clothing. You can shop locally for whatever you need in the way of sportswear, from golf and tennis gear to the world's widest selection of swimming costumes.

Miami swelters in summer, but air-conditioning systems can work overtime, blowing arctic air everywhere—in restaurants, office buildings, and shopping malls; on Metrobuses, Metrorail, and Metromover, the automated "people mover"—so always carry a wrap for the chilly indoors. Day and night, winter and summer, casual resort clothing is appropriate in Miami. Men needn't wear a tie or even a jacket, except to dine out at better restaurants in the evening. Older Latin men show a preference for the *guayabera,* the shirt-cum-jacket of the tropics, made to measure by Cuban tailors in Little Havana.

As for footwear, sandals may be worn all year round in South Florida, but you'll need a pair of sturdy closed shoes for nature walks and excursions to the Everglades. Don't forget to bring your sunglasses; they're a must in Miami, where the glare of high noon can be blinding. Other indispensables include sun visors or hats, and rubber sandals for the beach.

COMMUNICATIONS *(See also* HOURS*)*

Post offices. The U.S. postal service deals only with mail. Telephone and telegraph services are operated by other companies. The main post office for Greater Miami lies west of the airport at 2200 Milam Dairy Road, Miami, FL 33152; tel. (305) 599-1749.

You can purchase stamps from machines in post office entrance halls after closing time. Service is available after hours at the Miami International Airport facility, alongside the main terminal building. Post boxes are painted blue.

Poste restante (general delivery). You can have mail marked "General Delivery" sent to you care of the main post office. Letters will be held for up to a month. American Express offices also keep post for 30 days; envelopes should be marked "Client's Mail."

Take your driving licence or passport with you for identification.

Telegrams. American telegraph companies are run privately. They offer domestic and overseas services, as well as domestic telex facilities, and are listed in the *Yellow Pages*. You can telephone the telegraph office, dictate the message, and have the charge added to your hotel bill, or dictate it from a coin-operated phone and pay on the spot. A letter telegram (night letter) costs about half the standard rate.

Telephones. The independent American telephone systems are efficient and reliable. Phone boxes are found in the streets, at many service stations, in shopping plazas, in restaurants, and in most public buildings.

To make a local call, lift the receiver, put 35¢ in the appropriate slot, wait for the dialling tone, then dial the seven-digit number. For local information, ring 411. For local operator assistance, and for help within the same area code, dial "0."

Long-distance and many international calls may be dialled direct, even from a pay phone, if you follow the posted directions. If you don't know the correct area code, dial "00" for operator assistance. Long-distance calls cost more from a pay phone than from a private one.

Telephone rates are listed in the white pages of the telephone directory. Also included is information on personal, reverse-charge, and credit card calls. All numbers with an 800, 887, or 888 prefix are toll-free. Cheapest calls can be made from a private phone at night, during weekends, and on public holidays—when rates drop considerably.

Fax facilities. Major hotels have fax facilities, as do many stores.

COMPLAINTS

If you have a serious complaint about business practices in the Miami area and have talked to no avail with the manager of the establishment in question, contact the Consumer Protection Division of Dade County, 140 W. Flagler Street, Miami, FL; tel. (305) 375-4222; or the Agriculture Department, Consumer Services Division, The Capitol, Tallahassee, FL 32301; tel. (800) 435-7352. The head office serves as a clearing house for complaints and will refer callers to a Dade County number if necessary.

CONSULATES

Few English-speaking countries maintain a consulate in Florida.

Australia: 636 Fifth Avenue, New York; tel. (212) 245-4000.

Canada: 1251 Avenue of the Americas, New York; tel. (212) 586-2400.

Ireland: 515 Madison Avenue, New York; tel. (212) 319-2555.

New Zealand: Suite 530, 630 Fifth Avenue, New York; tel. (212) 586-0060.

South Africa: 333 East 38th Street, New York: tel. (212) 213 4880.

United Kingdom: 225 Peachtree Street N.E., Atlanta, Georgia; tel. (404) 524-5856.

CRIME

Visitors would be wise to take the same precautions here as they would in any other big city. Store valuables and reserves of cash in the hotel safe, carrying only enough with you for your daily needs. Beware of pickpockets, many of whom work in pairs. They frequent city buses, queues, crowded stores, and lifts.

To be on the safe side, go out after dark in a group, rather than alone, and leave your car with the attendant at a restaurant, night club, or discotheque, instead of parking it yourself on a dimly lit side street. If strangers try to stop you or if you become lost at night while you are driving, proceed to a well-lit area and ask for help at a service station or convenience store.

If you follow the normal common-sense rules of behaviour, you need not be apprehensive.

CUSTOMS and ENTRY FORMALITIES

Canadians need only proof of nationality to enter the United States. Citizens of the U.K. and most European countries need a passport and visa waiver only, but you should check with your travel agent or local U.S. embassy, as rules are complicated and subject to change. The application process can prove slow and difficult, depending on individual circumstances. When you apply, take along documents verifying your intention to return home.

A non-resident may bring into the U.S., free of duty and taxes, articles up to $100 in value intended as gifts for other people.

This exemption is valid only if the gifts accompany you—provided you stay 72 hours or more—and if you have not claimed the exemption during the preceding 6 months. A hundred cigars may be included within this gift exemption.

Plants and foodstuffs also are subject to strict control; visitors from abroad may not import fruit, vegetables, or meat. The same goes for chocolates that contain liqueur.

Passengers arriving or departing should declare any money or cheques exceeding $10,000.

Duty-free allowance. You will be asked to fill out a customs declaration form before you arrive in the U.S. The following chart shows what main duty-free items you may take into the U.S. (if you are over 21) and, when returning home, into your own country:

Into:	Cigarettes		Cigars		Tobacco	Spirits		Wine
U.S.	200	or	50	or	2 kg.	1 *l*	or	1 *l*
Australia	200	or	250 g.	or	250 g.	1 *l*	or	1 *l*
Canada	200	and	50	and	900 g.	1.14 *l*	or	1.14 *l*
Ireland	200	or	50	or	250 g.	1 *l*	and	2 *l*
New Zealand	200	or	50	or	½lb.	1 *qt.*	and	1 *qt.*
South Africa	400	and	50	and	250 g.	1 *l*	and	2 *l*
U.K.	200	or	50	or	250 g.	1 *l*	and	2 *l*

D

DRIVING

Drive on the right, overtake (pass) on the left. The speed limit is 15 mph in school zones, 30 mph in business or residential districts, 55 mph on motorways (highways), unless otherwise indicated. If you keep within the flow of traffic, you'll have no problem, but if you go any faster a patrol car will pull you over.

There are various types of motorway in Greater Miami: turnpikes are high-speed dual carriageways that collect tolls; expressways and interstate highways are usually free. Most maps indicate which roads collect tolls. It's a good idea to have a stock of coins on hand, as the "exact change" lanes move faster. Quarters are especially handy.

Avoid expressways and main thoroughfares during rush hours (7 to 9 a.m. and 4 to 6 p.m.), when traffic is reduced to a crawl.

Breakdowns. If you break down on a turnpike or expressway, pull over on to the right-hand shoulder, lift up the hood, and wait in the car (with doors locked!) for assistance. At night, use the hazard warning light. If your car is overheating, turn off the air conditioner—it's a strain on the engine.

Petrol (gas) and services. Many service stations have two "islands"—one for full service, the other for self service. You'll save money if you fill the tank yourself. The majority of stations close in the evenings and on Sundays.

Parking. Suburban malls and major tourist attractions provide ample free parking. At luxury malls, parking is cheaper with a "validated" ticket: any shopkeeper will stamp your ticket for you, even if you don't make a purchase. Many municipal car parks have meters; coins required and length of stay authorised are always indicated. In the city of Miami, parking can be difficult and expensive. If you plan to spend the day downtown, park your car at one of the outlying Metrorail stations and go into town by public transport. Be sure to park your car with, and not against, the flow of traffic. Do not park by a fire hydrant or alongside a kerb painted yellow.

Rules of the road. Florida state law requires motorists in both directions to come to a complete halt when a school bus stops to pick up or drop off children. Throughout Dade County, you may turn right when the traffic lights are red if there are no pedestrians on the crossing—and no signs to the contrary. Be sure to come to a complete stop first. Otherwise, international rules of the road apply.

American Automobile Association. The AAA offers assistance to members of affiliated organisations abroad. It also provides travel information for South Florida and can arrange car insurance by the month for owner-drivers. Contact Greater Miami AAA East Florida: 4770 Biscayne Boulevard, Miami, FL 33137; tel. (305) 571-0360.

Road signs. Although the U.S. is changing over to international pictographs, some differences remain between international and U.S. signs. Also, there are differences between British and U.S. terms:

Miami

American	British
American	*British*
Detour	Deviation
Divided highway	Dual carriageway
Expressway	Motorway
Men working	Roadworks
No passing	No overtaking
No parking along highway	Clearway
Railroad crossing	Level crossing
Traffic circle	Roundabout
Yield	Give way

DRUGS

Buying and selling hard drugs is a serious offence. Florida has a large force of undercover policemen who are battling to keep drugs out of the U.S.

E

ELECTRIC CURRENT

The U.S. has 110/115-volt 60-cycle A.C. Plugs are small, flat and two-pin; foreigners will need an adapter for razors and other appliances.

EMERGENCIES

Dial 911 to summon the police, an ambulance or the fire department.

The Emergency Room of Jackson Memorial Hospital at 1611 N.W. 12th Avenue in Miami will treat anyone in need of immediate attention.

G

GETTING THERE

Although the conditions described below have been carefully checked, it is advisable to consult a travel agent for the latest information on fares and other arrangements.

FROM NORTH AMERICA

By air: Greater Miami is easily accessible from the larger Northern, midwestern, and Western cities. There are many non-stop flights every day to Miami from New York, Chicago, Los Angeles, and San Francisco.

By bus: Miami is served by Greyhound/Trailways, Inc., coach.

By rail: Amtrak is currently advertising a variety of bargain fares, including Excursion and Family fares and tour packages with hotel and guide included.

By car: Travellers coming down the East Coast can take Interstate 95 via Washington and Atlanta. The toll turnpike system, another possibility, links up with the Sunshine State Parkway. The shortest route from the West Coast is Interstate 10, passing Tucson, El Paso, Houston, and Mobile.

FROM GREAT BRITAIN

By air: There are daily non-stop flights from Heathrow and Gatwick to Miami. Some U.S. airlines offer travellers from abroad a discount on the cost of each internal flight, or flat-rate unlimited-travel tickets for specific periods.

Charter flights and package tours: Many package tours are available, including camper holidays, coach tours, excursions to the Bahamas, trips to other American cities and sights, etc. Many Caribbean cruises originate in Miami, "cruise capital of the world."

Baggage. Baggage allowances for scheduled transatlantic flights are complex, but you are allowed to check in, free, two suitcases of normal size. In addition, one piece of hand baggage of a size which fits easily under the aircraft seat may be carried on board. Confirm size and weight restrictions with your travel agent or air carrier when booking your ticket.

It is advisable to insure all luggage for the duration of your trip. Any travel agent can make the necessary arrangements.

GUIDES and TOURS

The services of a tour guide are provided for the price of admission to various historic sites, including Cape Florida Lighthouse, Vizcaya, The Barnacle, and Coral Gables House. The Museum of Science employs "explainers"—university students who escort visitors around the exhibits on request.

Fairchild Tropical Garden operates hourly guided tram tours for an additional charge. Walking tours of the gardens, scheduled several times daily, are free.

Several different companies operate bus and boat tours to sights and attractions in Greater Miami. Helicopter tours are also available. Ask your hotel or any travel agency for information.

The Miami Design Preservation League offers tours of the Art Deco District on Saturdays at 10:30 a.m. and Thursdays at 6:30 p.m. Audio tours are available at the League's Welcome Center: 1001 Ocean Drive, Miami Beach. For details, phone (305) 672-2014.

In the national parks, rangers organise free nature walks, canoe trips, and the like. Inquire at the visitors' centres for details. Concessionaires also run tram tours of Shark Valley and boat trips from Flamingo in Everglades National Park.

Officially sponsored boat excursions to Elliot Key are available from Convoy Point in Biscayne National Park; you tour the park's reefs, bays, or islands with a park ranger at the helm. To make reservations, call Biscayne National Underwater Park, Inc., P.O. Box 1270, Homestead, FL 33030; tel. (305) 230-1100.

H

HEALTH and MEDICAL CARE (See also EMERGENCIES)

Foreign visitors should note that the United States doesn't provide free medical services, and medical treatment is expensive. Arrangements should therefore be made in advance for temporary health insurance (through a travel agent or an insurance company).

If you arrive in Miami after flying through several time zones, take it easy for the first couple of days. Doctors recommend eating lightly initially, and getting plenty of rest.

Beware of the Florida sun. Use a sun screen or complete-block cream at first, and build up a tan gradually, in small doses. Far too many tourists overdo it, ruining their holiday. Remember that second- and third-degree burns can result from over-exposure. Protect your eyes, too—the sun's ultra-violet rays can irritate the delicate tissues of the cornea, especially when reflected off the surface of the sea or pool.

Visitors from Britain will find that certain drugs sold over the counter at home can be purchased only on prescription in the U.S. There's no shortage of drug stores, or pharmacies, but only a few of them stay open late at night.

HITCH-HIKING

The FBI and police advise strongly against accepting rides from strangers, and it is illegal on all highways.

HOURS

Offices in Greater Miami open from 9 a.m. to 5 p.m. Monday to Friday, and banks from 9 a.m. until 2 p.m. (later at the airport). Post offices open from 8:30 a.m. to 5 p.m. Monday to Friday, till noon only on Saturdays. The airport facility provides service until 9 p.m. from Monday to Friday, till 12:30 p.m. on Saturdays.

Shops and department stores in central Miami and most other municipalities do business from 9 or 10 a.m. to 5:30 or 6 p.m., Monday to Saturday. However, most of the luxury malls and suburban shopping centres have extended hours, operating daily from 10 a.m. until 9 or 9:30 p.m. and from noon to 5 or 6:30 on Sundays. There are exceptions to this general rule. Certain centres may close several nights a week and others may open Sunday mornings, so it's a good idea to telephone before you make a special trip.

Restaurants generally serve lunch from 11 a.m. to 1:30 p.m., dinner from 5 p.m. to 10 or 11 p.m. (even midnight and after at a few places, especially on Calle Ocho). Fast-food outlets open from 6:30 a.m. (7:30 Sundays) to midnight or 1 a.m. A few coffee shops provide 24-hour service.

Most tourist attractions open their doors seven days a week from 9 or 10 a.m. to 5 or 6 p.m. The ticket windows at the Seaquarium, Planet Ocean, and Metrozoo shut 1½ hours before closing time.

L

LANGUAGE

Spanish runs a close second to English in Miami, with its burgeoning Hispanic community. In some parts of the city, especially downtown, Little Havana, and Hialeah, you may be addressed in

Spanish first and then English, particularly by members of the older generation or by new arrivals from south of the border. For a time, Miami declared itself a bilingual city, but the emphasis nowadays is on English.

You'll hear some Yiddish spoken in the southern reaches of Miami Beach, home to a fair number of Jewish-Americans of Eastern European origin, while Creole holds sway in Little Haiti, making Miami a truly cosmopolitan city.

Some English-speaking foreigners are perplexed by certain American words and phrases. The following are a few that cause confusion:

U.S.	British	U.S.	British
admission	entry fee	**pavement**	road surface
bathroom	toilet (private)	**purse/**	
bill	note (money)	**pocketbook**	handbag
billfold	wallet	**rest room**	toilet
check	bill (restaurant)	**round-trip**	return (ticket)
collect call	reverse-charge	**second floor**	first floor
	call	**sidewalk**	pavement
dead end	cul-de-sac	**stand in line**	queue up
elevator	lift	**trailer**	caravan
first floor	ground floor	**underpass**	subway
gasoline	petrol	**vest**	waistcoat
liquor	spirits	**wash up**	wash oneself
liquor store	off-licence	**windshield**	windscreen
minister	clergyman	**yard**	garden

LOST PROPERTY

If you lose something in a public building, chances are it will be turned in to the "lost and found department." Restaurants and taxi companies hold lost articles in the hope that someone will retrieve them. Should you leave something behind on public transport, be it bus or rail, call (305) 375-3366. Otherwise, contact the police department in the municipality where the loss occurred. Report the loss of your passport to the nearest consulate as well (see page 113).

M

MAPS

Miami is changing so quickly, it's essential to procure a current town plan. Available in book shops, the Rand McNally map of Miami and Miami Beach takes in all 27 of the Greater Miami municipalities. The South Florida Map Company publishes an excellent plan of Miami and Metropolitan Dade County, including individual maps of Miami and Coral Gables. The Chamber of Commerce in each municipality distributes free maps, as does the Greater Miami Convention & Visitors Bureau.

Any marine supplier and most book shops carry up-to-date navigation charts prepared by the National Ocean Survey. Chart 11467 gives full details of offshore waters from Elliott Key north to Lake Worth.

The maps included in this guide were prepared by GeoSystems Global Corp.

MEETING PEOPLE

Like most Americans, the people of Miami are friendly, open, and easy to meet. Miamians will quickly spot a foreigner and start to chat, inquiring about your accent, where you're from, where you're staying, how you like their city. Perhaps the best place to make new friends is around the hotel pool, but you'll find yourself coming into contact with people almost everywhere—waiting in a queue, visiting a museum, or shopping for a swimming costume.

MONEY MATTERS

Currency. The dollar is divided into 100 cents.

Bank notes: $1, $2 (rare), $5, $10, $20, $50, and $100. Larger denominations are not in general circulation. All notes are the same shape and colour, so it's easy to confuse them. Try to separate large and small denominations.

Coins: 1¢ (called a "penny"), 5¢ ("nickel"), 10¢ ("dime"), 25¢ ("quarter"), 50¢ ("half dollar"), and $1. You may inadvertently be given Canadian or other foreign coins in change. Canadian coins are worth about 15% less than U.S. ones, and they do not work in automatic machines, such as telephones.

Banks and currency exchange (See also HOURS). Very few branch banks change foreign currency. Unless you are planning to go downtown, Miami International Airport is probably the most convenient place to make transactions. Some hotels change money, but the rate is not advantageous. It is simpler to carry dollar traveller's cheques (see below) or major credit cards.

When changing money or traveller's cheques, ask for $20 notes, which are accepted everywhere; some establishments refuse larger notes unless they nearly equal the amount to be paid.

Credit cards. When buying goods or tickets and paying hotel or phone bills, you will be asked: "Cash or charge?," meaning you have the choice of paying in cash or by credit card. Businesses are wary of little-known credit cards, but they'll gladly accept major American or international cards.

Many service stations and other businesses will not take money at night, only cards. Outside normal office hours, it's sometimes impossible to hire cars and pay bills with cash.

You'll need to show some form of identification when charging your purchase.

Traveller's cheques. Visitors from abroad may find traveller's cheques drawn on American banks easier to cash than those on foreign banks. Cash small amounts at a time, keeping the balance of your cheques in the hotel safe if possible. It's a good idea to follow instructions given for recording where and when you cashed each cheque.

Prices. In Greater Miami, most prices do not include a state sales tax of 6.5%. Hotels add 11.5%–12.5% to the bill.

The U.S. has a larger range of prices for the same item than you will find anywhere else, as well as a greater choice of goods. For moderately priced articles, visit the big department stores. Small independent grocery stores, drugstores, and 24-hour "convenience stores" have higher prices, but independent service stations are cheaper than those of the large oil companies.

PLANNING YOUR BUDGET

To help plan your budget, here's a list of approximate prices in U.S. dollars—but bear in mind that prices are subject to change.

Airport transfer. Taxi to central Coral Gables $17, to downtown Miami $20, to Port of Miami $15.75, to Miami Beach up to $25.

Attractions. Seaquarium $19.95 adults; Parrot Jungle $12.95 adults, $7; Fairchild Tropical Garden $8; Vizcaya $10; The Barnacle $1.

Babysitter. $4–5 per hour for one or two children, $1 for each additional child, plus transport expenses. Hotels charge $6–8 per hour.

Bicycle hire. $5–7 per hour, $15 per day, $35 per week (for a three-speed).

Camping. From $6 per day, per site.

Car hire. Rates vary considerably with the company and the season. By way of comparison, the price of a mid-size car is $175 per week, $25 per day.

Cigarettes (20), $2.30; higher for foreign brands.

Entertainment. Cinema $6–8, nightclub/discotheque $5–20 cover charges, $4–6 drinks.

Hairdressers. Man's haircut $7–25; Woman's haircut $12–50, cut, shampoo, and set $20–30, colour rinse/dye $50–100.

Hotels. Double room with bath: deluxe from $250, moderate $125–250, budget under $125.

Meals and drinks. Continental breakfast $2–5, full breakfast $4–10, lunch in snack bar $5, in restaurant $7.50–14, dinner $15–30 (more with entertainment), coffee $1, espresso $1.50–2, beer $2.50–3, glass of wine $2.50–4, carafe $6–9, bottle from $10, cocktail $3.50–6.

Metrobus. Local $1.25, express $1.50, transfer 25¢.

Metrorail. $1.25 tokens, 10 for $10 .

Metromover. 25¢.

Taxis. $1, plus $1.75 per mile.

N

NEWSPAPERS and MAGAZINES

Two daily papers are published in Greater Miami: the *Miami Herald* and its Spanish-language edition, *El Nuevo Herald,* widely read throughout the Americas, and *Diario Las Americas,* aimed at a growing Hispanic readership in the United States. The weekly *New Times* features arts and entertainment highlights.

Miami

You can purchase local newspapers and the daily *USA Today* from street-corner vending machines and at newsstands (often in drugstores and convenience stores). Larger newsstands and vending machines in certain locations carry *The New York Times, Wall Street Journal,* and a selection of other American papers. The London Sunday papers are available several days after publication at a few larger newsstands (refer to the *Yellow Pages* under "News Dealers").

Supermarkets and newsstands all over Miami carry a selection of national and international magazines, as well as the local *Miami Metro* which features a calendar of events, and the very fashionable, society-oriented.

P

PHOTOGRAPHY

Camera shops sell film, but drugstores and supermarkets supply the same at discount prices. Do not leave film anywhere in the car: it will be ruined in the heat.

Airport security machines may damage film. Ask for it to be checked separately, or buy a film shield.

POLICE

City police are concerned with local crime and traffic offences. Highway Patrol officers (also called State Troopers) ensure highway safety and are on the lookout for people speeding or driving under the influence of alcohol or drugs.

Don't hesitate to approach any police officer for information or assistance; helping you is part of their job.

The police emergency number is 911.

PUBLIC HOLIDAYS

If a holiday, such as Christmas Day, falls on a Sunday, banks and most stores close the following day. There are also long weekends (e.g., the one following Thanksgiving) when offices are closed for four days. Many restaurants never shut, however, even at Christmas.

New Year's Day	January 1
Martin Luther King Day	Third Monday in January

Washington's Birthday*	Third Monday in February
Memorial Day	Last Monday in May
Independence Day	July 4
Labor Day	First Monday in September
Columbus Day*	Second Monday in October
Veterans' Day	November 11
Thanksgiving Day	Fourth Thursday in November
Christmas Day	December 25

* Shops and businesses open

R

RADIO and TV

Miami has several dozen AM and FM radio stations, broadcasting everything from country, Latin, and rock to rhythm-and-blues. Some stations feature religious programmes, others are dedicated to talk, and there are those that broadcast in Spanish only. There's one classical-music radio station, WTMI, 93.1 F.M. on the dial.

Local news and sports programmes can be seen at 6 p.m., followed by national and international news at 6:30 or 7, and again at 11 p.m. The shows produced by the major American networks are the staple of Miami television, though local offerings in Spanish and English provide a regional flavour. There are no commercials on the educational Public Broadcasting Service (channel 2), which produces its own excellent news and information programmes, in addition to music, dance, and natural-science features. Cable television, available in many hotels and motels, gives access to several dozen channels.

For a list of weekly television programmes, consult *TV Guide,* sold at newsstands everywhere, or the TV magazines published by the *Miami Herald* (Sunday), which also carries radio information.

RELIGIOUS SERVICES

Saturday newspapers publish information about religious services. Miami has numerous synagogues, as well as Protestant, Roman-Catholic, and Greek-Orthodox churches, and other places of worship.

T

TIME and DATES

The continental United States has a total of four time zones; Florida (like New York) is on Eastern Standard Time. In summer (between April and October) Daylight Saving Time is adopted and clocks move ahead an hour.

The following chart shows the time in various cities in winter when it's noon in Miami:

Los Angeles	**Miami**	London	Sydney
9 a.m.	**noon**	5 p.m.	4 a.m.
Sunday	**Sunday**	Sunday	Monday

For the exact time, call (305) 324-8811.

Dates in the U.S. are written in a different form from that of Britain; for example, 1/6/99 means January 6, 1999.

TIPPING

Waiters and waitresses earn most of their wages from tips; often they are paid little else. Restaurants do not normally add a service charge. Cinema and theatre ushers and petrol station attendants do not expect anything extra.

Here are some suggestions for tipping:

Porter, per bag	50¢–$1 (minimum $1)
Hotel maid, per week	$3–5
Waiter	15%
Lavatory attendant	25¢
Taxi driver	15%
Guide	10–15%
Hairdresser/Barber	15%

TOILETS

You will find toilets in most public buildings, including department stores, theatres, and petrol stations. Public beaches and large recreational parks usually provide toilet facilities. In some places you have to pay; in others you should leave a tip for the attendant.

Recommended Hotels

Still growing as a holiday destination, Miami offers a large choice of accommodations. Competition in the highly developed hospitality industry means that you'll be assured of value for money, no matter what kind of establishment you choose. Here we can only make a small selection. Each entry is marked with a series of stars indicating the price range, per night, of a double room with bath, excluding breakfast. Tax of about 11.5%–12.5% is added to hotel bills.

In the U.S., rates are quoted for the room, not per person. Additional occupants over two may be charged a small premium. A few places include a simple Continental breakfast. Always ask about special rate packages, e.g., for stays of a few days, lower midweek rates, and off-season rates.

✪	below $125
✪✪	$125–$250
✪✪✪	$250 and over

The Alexander ✪✪✪ *5225 Collins Avenue, Miami Beach, FL 33140; tel. (305) 865-6500, fax (305) 864-8525.* Luxury suites in pink tower near its own wide beach. Landscaped gardens and pools. 211 rooms.

Avalon Majestic Hotel ✪✪ *700 Ocean Drive, Miami Beach, FL 33139; tel. (305) 538-0133/ (800) 933-3306, fax (305) 534-0258.* Art-Deco glamour on the beach, with decor that will take you back to the 1930s. 106 rooms.

Astor Hotel ✪✪ *956 Washington Avenue, Miami Beach, FL 33139; tel. (305) 531-8081/ (800) 270-4981, fax (305) 531-3193.* Though recently remodeled, this hotel retains much of its original charm. Excellent service; 42 small but beautifully elegant rooms.

Bay Harbor Inn ✪✪ *9601 E. Bay Harbor Drive, Bay Harbor Island, FL 33154; tel. (305) 868-4141, fax (305) 867-9094.* Steps away from the beach, this little hotel is one of the island's best-kept secrets. 38 rooms, 10 suites.

Best Western Miami Airport Inn ✪✪ *1550 N.W. Lejeune Road, Miami, FL 33126; tel. (305) 871-2345, fax (305) 871-2811.* Reasonable economy near international airport. Pool. 209 rooms.

Biscayne Bay Marriott ✪✪/✪✪✪ *1633 N. Bayshore Drive, Miami, FL 33132; tel. (305) 374-3900 or (800) 228-9290, fax (305) 375-0597.* Downtown bayfront hotel adjoining shopping mall. Pool. 584 rooms.

Casa Grande Suite Hotel ✪✪✪ *834 Ocean Drive, Miami Beach, FL 33139; tel. (305) 672-7003/ (800) OUTPOST, fax (305) 673-3669.* The epitome of South Beach luxury, yet the atmosphere is relaxed and comfortable. Excellent service, stylish rooms, ocean views, all the amenities. 34 suites.

Colony ✪✪ *736 Ocean Drive, Miami Beach, FL 33139; tel. (305) 673-0088 or (800) 226-5669, fax (305) 532-0762.* Art-Deco treasure, restored and now a focus of fashionable South Beach. 36 rooms.

Delano ✪✪✪ *1685 Collins Avenue, Miami Beach, FL 33139; tel. (305) 672-2000/ (800) 555-5001, fax (305) 532-0099.* This recently renovated, elegant hotel is a South Beach hot spot. 208 rooms and suites.

Doubletree ✪✪ *2649 S. Bayshore Drive, Coconut Grove, FL 33133; tel. (305) 858-2500 or (800) 872-7749, fax (305) 858-2776.* Spacious rooms with views of the bay and the "Grove." Pool, tennis. 192 rooms.

Essex House ✪✪ *1001 Collins Avenue, Miami Beach, FL 33139; tel. (305) 534-2700/ (800) 553-7739, fax (305) 532-*

3827. The building is an Art-Deco landmark, with many original, restored architectural details and furnishings. One block from the ocean, 62 rooms, 19 suites.

Fontainebleau Hilton ✪✪✪ *4441 Collins Avenue, Miami Beach, FL 33140; tel. (305) 538-2000 or (800) 548-8886, fax (305) 674-4607.* Huge white curving blocks in lush grounds next to the beach. Pools, tennis. 1204 rooms.

Grand Bay ✪✪✪ *2669 S. Bayshore Drive, Coconut Grove, FL 33133; tel. (305) 858-9600 or (800) 327-2788, fax (305) 859-2026.* Spacious, architecturally winning luxury overlooking Biscayne Bay. Pool. 181 rooms.

Hotel Inter-Continental Miami ✪✪✪ *100 Chopin Plaza, Miami. FL 33131; tel. (305) 577-1000/ (800) 327-3005, fax (305) 577-0384.* The nicest hotel in the Financial District. Three restaurants, plus every imaginable amenity. 646 rooms.

Hotel Place St. Michel ✪✪ *162 Alcazar Avenue, Coral Gables, FL 33134; tel. (305) 444-1666/ (800) 848-HOTEL, fax (305) 529-0074.* Those in the know come again and again to this little bit of Europe in Coral Gables. Beautiful furnishings, excellent service. 27 rooms.

Mayfair House ✪✪✪ *3000 Florida Avenue, Coconut Grove, FL 33133; tel. (305) 441-0000 or (800) 433-4555, fax 447-9173.* All-suite hotel in the very heart of the "Grove." Pool, views. 179 suites.

Ocean Front Hotel ✪✪ *1230-38 Ocean Drive, Miami Beach, FL 33139; tel. (305) 672-2579, fax (305) 672-7665.* Service and ambience are very French, with pleasant rooms and ocean views. 27 rooms and suites.

Park Washington Hotel ✪✪ *1020 Washington Avenue, Miami Beach, FL 33139; tel. (305) 532-1930, fax (305) 672-6706.* Inexpensive South Beach lodgings in a building designed in the 1930s. Pool, kitchenettes. 30 rooms.

Miami

Riande Continental Bayside ✪✪ *146 Biscayne Boulevard, Miami, FL 33132; tel. (305) 358-4555/ (800) RIANDE-1, fax (305) 371-5253.* Ideal shopping location steps away from bayside, great ethnic restaurants, and a Metrorail stop. 250 rooms.

Sheraton Bal Harbour Beach Resort ✪✪✪ *9701 Collins Avenue, Bal Harbour, FL 33154; tel. (305) 865-7511 or (800) 325-3535, fax (305) 864-2601.* Landscaped resort on the ocean. Tennis, pools, golf. 642 rooms.

Sonesta Beach Resort ✪✪✪ *350 Ocean Drive, Key Biscayne, FL 33149; tel. (305) 361-2021 or (800) 766-3782, fax (305) 361-3096.* Family-oriented resort on the ocean. Tennis, pools, golf course adjoining. 300 rooms.

Suez Oceanfront Resort ✪ *18215 Collins Avenue, Sunny Isles, FL 33160; tel. (305) 932-0661/ (800) 327-5278, fax (305) 937-0058.* Kitschy hotel with interesting decor, including a replica of the Sphinx, but an excellent value. Pool, tennis courts, exercise room with sauna. 198 rooms.

Turnberry Isle Yacht & Country Club ✪✪✪ *19999 W. Country Club Drive, Aventura, FL 33180; tel. (305) 932-6200 or (800) 327-7028, fax 933-6560.* Elegant resort with ocean club, pools, golf courses. 357 rooms.

Westin Resort ✪✪✪ *4833 Collins Avenue, Miami Beach, FL 33140; tel. (305) 532-3600, fax 532-2334, fax for guests 534-7409.* Tower on the ocean. Comprehensive fitness facilities, tennis, pool, boating, golf nearby. 423 rooms.

Wyndham Hotel ✪✪ *1601 Biscayne Boulevard, Miami, FL 33132; tel. (305) 374-0000/ (800) 996-3426, fax (305) 374-0020.* Full-service, contemporary hotel. Pool, health club, sauna, conference rooms. 528 rooms and suites.

Recommended Restaurants

Everywhere you turn, there's somewhere to eat, almost always open seven days a week. Here we give a selection of full-service restaurants, buffet restaurants, and food courts (multiple outlets sharing a table area). There is no space to list even a fraction of the vast number of restaurants and all-you-can-eat buffets well within our lowest price range. (See also the section on Eating Out in the main part of this guide, page 93.)

Each entry is marked with a symbol indicating the price range, per person, for a dinner comprising starter or salad, main course, and dessert. (Drinks, gratuities, and 6.5%–7.5% sales tax are not included.)

✪	up to $15
✪✪	$15-30
✪✪✪	$30 and over

Café Abbracci ✪✪✪ *318 Aragon Avenue, Coral Gables; tel. (305) 441-0700.* Northern Italian cuisine; perfect seafood dishes and a friendly atmosphere.

Casa Juancho ✪✪ *2436 S.W. 8th Street, Little Havana; tel. (305) 642-2452.* Fine Spanish and Cuban food, featuring *tapas* and regional entrées; strolling musicians entertain nightly.

Chef Allen's ✪✪✪ *19088 N.E. 29th Avenue, Aventura; tel. (305) 935-2900.* Former Le Cirque chef Allen Susser's latest venue. Tempting New-World entrées and an excellent wine list.

The Crepe Maker ✪ *70 S. Biscayne Boulevard, Downtown; tel. (305) 233-1113.* Two sidewalk carts offering healthy, fresh meats and vegetables wrapped in crêpes.

Miami

Don Schula's Restaurant ✪✪✪ *5225 Collins Avenue, Miami Beach; tel. (305) 865-6500.* Steakhouse with an á la carte menu and an excellent selection of seafood.

Grillfish ✪ *1444 Collins Avenue, South Beach; tel. (305) 538-9908.* Reasonably-priced seafood menu and elegant decor make this place a favorite with the locals.

Islas Canarias ✪ *285 N.W. 27th Avenue, Miami; tel. (305) 649-0440.* Popular traditional Cuban cooking in Little Havana area. No credit cards.

Joe's Stone Crab ✪✪ *227 Biscayne Street, Miami Beach; tel. (305) 673-0365.* An institution since 1913, open from October to May.

La Boulangerie ✪ *328 Crandon Boulevard, Key Biscayne; tel. (305) 361-0281.* Small French bakery with surprisingly good sandwiches, salads, and pastries.

Larios on the Beach ✪ *820 Ocean Drive, Miami Beach; tel. (305) 532-9577.* Rich variety of Cuban food dished up by Gloria Estefan's favorite chef, who she imported from Cuba.

Le Pavillon ✪✪✪ *100 Chopin Plaza (in the Hotel Inter-Continental); tel. (305) 372-4494.* Very exclusive restaurant serving New-World cuisine with a regional flair.

Malaga ✪ *740 S.W. 8th Street, Miami; tel. (305) 858-4224.* Traditional Cuban and Spanish dishes on "Calle Ocho."

The Nemo Restaurant ✪✪✪ *100 Collins Avenue, South Beach; tel. (305) 532-4550.* Noisy hot-spot with a model-and-actor crowd, an excellent wait-staff, and multicultural cuisine.

Norman's ✪✪✪ *21 Almera Avenue, Coral Gables; tel. (305) 446-6767.* Tasteful, comfortable atmosphere; Asian- and Caribbean-influenced cuisine served from an open kitchen.

Osteria del Teatro ✪✪✪ *1443 Washington Avenue, South Beach; tel. (305) 538-7850.* Locals and tourists clamor for the handmade pastas at this reliable Northern Italian restaurant. Ask the waiter to recommend a daily special.

The Palm ✪✪✪ *9650 E. Bay Harbor Drive, Bay Harbor Island; tel. (305) 868-7256.* Dark steakhouse known for large portions and equally large prices.

Los Ranchos ✪✪ *Bayside Marketplace, Miami; tel. (305) 375-0666.* Nicaraguan-style steakhouse.

Rascal House ✪ *17190 Collins Avenue, North Miami Beach; tel. (305) 947-4581.* New-York-style deli known for its hearty sandwiches and large portions.

The Red Lantern ✪✪ *3176 Commodore Plaza, Coconut Grove; tel. (305) 529-9998.* Interesting, original Cantonese dishes in a low-key atmosphere.

Rusty Pelican ✪✪ *3201 Rickenbacker Causeway, Key Biscayne; tel. (305) 361-3818.* Very romantic dining room, complete with a waterfall. American entrées, such as steak and lobster. Go for the view of the city at sunset.

Sakura ✪ *8225 S.W. 124th Street, Miami; tel. (305) 238-8462.* Sushi, tempura, teriyaki dishes.

Señor Frog's ✪ *3480 Main Highway, Coconut Grove; tel. (305) 448-0999.* Kid-friendly Mexican restaurant serving huge portions in a cheerful, raucous atmosphere.

Miami

Sheldon's Drugs ✪ *9501 Harding Avenue, Surfside; tel (305) 866-6251.* An American drug-store counter serving breakfast and tasty blue-plate specials at 1960s prices.

Shorty's ✪ *9200 Dixie Highway, South Miami; tel. (305) 670-7732.* The best, melt-in-your-mouth chicken and ribs in Miami.

Smith and Wollensky Restaurant ✪✪ *1 Washington Avenue, South Beach; tel. (305) 673-1708.* New-York-style steakhouse with all the trimmings.

Sport Café ✪ *538 Washington Avenue, South Beach; tel. (305) 674-9700.* Family-run restaurant and bar with an authentic Italian menu. Large portions, excellent pastas and bread.

The Tea Room ✪ *12310 S.W. 224th Street, Goulds; tel. (305) 258-0044.* An oasis of English civility and sweet desserts close to a small enclave of art and antiques stores.

Versailles ✪ *3555 S.W. 8th Street, Little Havana; tel. (305) 444-0240.* Cuban diner serving tasty, simple food like beans and rice, *ropa vieja,* and good *cafe con leche*.

Wolfie Cohen's Rascal House ✪ *17190 Collins Avenue, Sunny Isles; tel. (305) 947-4581.* A fixture in Miami Beach since 1954. Large portions of Jewish deli specialties such as chicken soup and corned beef; eat in or take-out.

WPA ✪✪ *685 Washington Avenue, Miami; tel. (305) 534-1684.* Relaxed bistro-style modern American cooking with Italian and Tex-Mex variations.

Yuca ✪✪✪ *501 Lincoln Road, Miami; tel. (305) 532-9822.* Upscale, advanced Cuban cuisine in an elegant setting.